Kudos for The Perfect Fit

"I have tears in my eyes just thinking about reviewing this book! I can't say enough about it—it so changed my life the first time I read it and continues to do so each time thereafter. The author has such a way with putting God, dating, and life all in one basket. I would suggest this book if you're single, dating or even married—a must read!" Cameron Miller

"This book is a page turner from start to finish. The writer's style is so open, and honest and you can feel the vulnerability in every page. It's a must read if you have been divorced and are lost and looking for love again. There is hope for all of us who are suffering in pain and loss. I am sure you will be as touched by this book as I have been." Carrie Knight

"I thought I was going to read a book that would make me feel bad about my mistakes and even guilty about my life. I didn't want to read a book about two incredible people who have this perfect relationship and how God blessed them time and again. I didn't want to read victory where I had failed. I did not get any of this from your book—I actually received hope." James Raber

"This book literally changed my life. It's filled with so much anticipation and emotion; it could easily be a work of fiction. But praise God it isn't! It will compel anyone who reads it to give their heart, life, and future to God, showing He can be trusted to keep His promises. I cry every time I open it to read more, because I feel like I'm reading my own struggles, flaws, thoughts, and feelings. It has given me new hope and confidence to lay EVERYTHING at God's feet, even when it seems that nothing is happening." Diana Matthews

"I couldn't put your book down...it down it made me feel as though I was reading about my own life. Thank you for sharing and being honest while God was working every detail in your lives. Your book has given me hope that truly God has not forgotten me." Meika Jones

"I have to tell you that I got your book on Friday and was finished with it by Sunday. I laughed and cried throughout the whole book. It was such an awesome story of how God works with us when we are obedient." Debra Duffy

"I recently bought your book and let me tell you it is the best book I have read this year. It has really inspired me in many different ways. After being divorced, this book has encouraged me to keep going forward. It has been a wake up call from God to stop what I am doing." Gabby Silva

"I read Julie's book in one sitting. I saw so many parallels to my own experiences that I couldn't put it down." Haley

"I can't tell you all the encouragement and inspiration I have drawn from your book. I have read it three times now, each time with new hope, strength, and inspiration. You have touched lives in Africa..." Fonnie Dickson—Nigeria

"A stellar read! Not bored for one second! I laughed, cried and went through so many emotions...even weeks after reading it I am still going through emotions and digesting it all. God stirred something in me to believe again. I had really gotten in a rut in this area of my life, but the white rose made me think again and made me want a love adventure of my own. Get your hands on it today and then share it!" F.G.

"This book touched me personally on very many levels. I appreciated the candor as I could relate to the feelings of guessing, questioning and wondering as we all do. Julie's sense of humor is uplifting and encouraging as are her frustrations, knowing that it happens to the best of us! I recommend this book to all who dare to love. Dare to trust God for one of the most important decisions of your life. Your hopes for true love will be inspired." Robin Jones

"It was amazing how much I could relate to this book. Completely trusting the Lord for your mate...and trusting every step of the journey. Julie is a gifted writer, and her sense of humor keeps it real, which made it very hard to put the book down. I found myself laughing, crying, and reflecting several times. I felt like I was right there walking every step with her in this AMAZING, divinely-inspired love journey. I recommend this book to anyone who is single and waiting for their perfect fit. This book will give you hope if you have none, and show you that you are not alone! Great book!!" B. Ojala

"Thank you Julie for writing your testimony and sharing it with the world, and giving so many of us hope—hope in love, second chances and yet another reason to put our trust in God, who makes possible the impossible. I'm so grateful to you for writing this book for divorced women and/or single moms and the desire we have for a godly man in our lives who will treasure and cherish us, and love our children as their own." N. Celestine

"I could NOT put this book down. It was a fantastic read and it hit me hardcore. This book is a MUST read for every teen in a youth group and every young adult in a singles ministry and every middle aged person thinking they have failed in love. God KNEW I would need this book and He gave me this gift from Julie at the perfect time!" Nicci

The Perfect Fit

Piecing together true love...

Julie Ferwerda

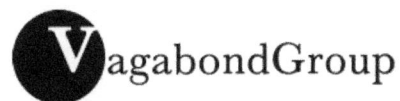

The Perfect Fit: Piecing Together True Love

© 2019 2nd revised edition, by Julie A. Ferwerda. All rights reserved.

© 2004 1st edition, by Julie Ferwerda. All rights reserved.

Vagabond Group LLC (PO Box 801, Rathdrum, ID 83858 USA). Design, content, editorial accuracy, and views expressed or implied in this work are those of the author. Publisher contact information: JulieFerwerda.com.

ISBN 978-0-9843578-6-4

No portion of this book may be reproduced, stored in a retrieval system, or transmitted in any form or by any means—electronic, mechanical, photocopy, recording, or any other—except for brief quotations in printed reviews, without prior permission in writing from the author/publisher.

Scripture quotations, unless otherwise indicated, are taken from the HOLY BIBLE, NEW INTERNATIONAL VERSION®. NIV®. Copyright ©1973, 1978, 1984 by International Bible Society. All rights reserved.

Other Scripture quotations are from the following source:

The Holy Bible, New Living Translation (NLT), copyright © 1996, Tyndale House Publishers, Inc., Wheaton, Illinois. All rights reserved.

Printed in the United States of America.

Love \ Romance \ Relationships \ Singles

Dedication & Acknowledgements

This book is dedicated to the loving memory of a praying Mom. Though she never saw the answer to her prayers with her eyes, she saw them with her heart.

Marian Gailbreath Ferwerda
Born November 15, 1930
Died February 3, 1999

And to another Mom who walked a good part of this journey with us. The world is a lot less sunshiny without her in our daily lives, but her generous heart and loving smile are always with us.
Molly West Browall
Born January 10, 1940
Died June 19, 2009

Also to Dani and Jessi, the most amazing, talented, loving daughters any parents could wish for! Our continued prayers for you are that you find men who inspire you and empower you toward the highest versions of yourselves and make you feel fully loved, appreciated, and safe.

Thanks to all the many people who contributed to the making of this story. Your parts in the divine plan will always be remembered and cherished.

And a big thank you to Shucks, my "perfect fit," for being willing to let me tell the story the way I saw it. You are such a great sport. Twenty years and a heck of a lot of life behind us, the reward for waiting has been better than I ever dreamed! Love you forever. P.S. As I encouraged in the 1st edition, I think hiring a couple bodyguards before this hits the shelves might still be a good move.

Table of Contents

FOREWORD 9
STEP 1: STARTING ON THE TABLE OF HOPE .. 11
STEP 2: ASSEMBLING THE BORDER 47
STEP 3: FILLING IN THE MIDDLE 65
STEP 4: PLACING THE LAST PIECE 143
EPILOGUE RESTORED DREAMS 167

Foreword

> Since ancient times no one has heard, no ear has perceived, no eye has seen any God besides you, who acts on behalf of those who wait for Him. You come to the help of those who gladly do right, who remember your ways. Isaiah 64:4-5

Do you wonder if there are second chances after divorce or broken relationships? Does pure, lasting romance really exist? Do you want to believe God can fix any mess you have made and bring a fulfilling, purposeful plan into your life in spite of your mistakes? If you have answered yes to any of these questions, then this book is for you.

No matter what mistakes have been made in the past, singles coming out of divorce or failed relationships can have hope of a second chance for a beautiful, divinely inspired romance. This book uses a step-by-step jigsaw puzzle analogy to show how God can take the broken and jumbled pieces of your life, and turn them into a beautiful picture. How do I know?

He did it for me, and He can do the same for you. In the following pages, you'll find out how an inspiring, many-pieced jigsaw puzzle came together, giving me an inspiring second chance at godly romance. My story, woven throughout the pages of this book, demonstrates God's goodness, and brings assurance through personal example that the important details of our lives are not left to chance.

As my picture is put together piece by piece, hopefully you'll experience newfound hope in God's personal attention to the details of your life in a deeply moving and intimate way. I pray that my story will give you the patience to believe He can and will prepare an exciting love adventure for anyone who is willing to trust Him, regardless of whether it involves a romantic relationship or not. It is my greatest desire that you are ready and willing to discover the wonderful adventure God has planned just for you.

2019: The benefit of reading the updated version of this book, exactly twenty years after the story began, is that I can most definitely assure you that the God who authored this love story has indeed been abundantly faithful to every single one of His promises.

On page 121, I detail the promise that God gave me during the most insecure time of my life: that He would continually pour His unfailing love into Steve's heart for me throughout all the days of our lives (this will become very significant as you read the precarious details in the coming pages), and that I could fully put my trust in this God-inspired love story after a first failed marriage. We've had a truly incredible two decades together, with the best of our story commencing at the end of this book (sequel alert!).

Our views and beliefs have changed significantly over the course of our lives together, but not our faith in a good God. We cannot say with certainty that there is "one God's best" for every person, as it seems that God works very differently in people's lives. Please don't get too caught up in putting God in any boxes, as He is the author of creativity and storytelling His way. But He is worth trusting with every detail!

In addition, everyone's path is different and no one should feel shame or judgment from this book. This was written based on where we were at in our faith and beliefs at that point in our lives, but people's beliefs should be expected to change and improve over time, as we grow more deeply in our understanding of God and life. Having said that, we still wouldn't change one detail about our story and experience. It was a perfect fit for us. And now I'm just as excited to share it with you as I was the day of my first publication. Let's get started!

Step 1: Starting on the Table of Hope

In the spring of 1997 all I could see of my life was a big muddled mess of shapes and colors waiting to be pieced together. But before that could happen, I needed a sturdy table that was large enough to support the entire project. There had to be a flat, unmoving, safe surface to prevent disaster. Hope in a good God, creator of dreams and dreamers, is just that! This foundation won't move, sway back and forth, change, or collapse, and it cultivates our trust and belief in the process. Join me now to watch as an inspiring puzzle is arranged, piece by piece.

The Perfect Fit

Swing the Stick
(Aim for Divine Promises)

"Will you be traveling first class or economy class?" the agent asked me over the phone, trying to help me book my airline ticket.

I knew what I wished the answer could be. I mean, who wouldn't want to travel first class? I'd been traveling economy all my life—crowded seats, cranky flight attendants, not enough pillows. And these days, add extra for luggage fees and a little baggy of pretzels (if you're lucky).

On my occasional glance beyond the holy veil into first class section, however, I've noticed something quite different—something I could only dream of on my limited resources. People—happy, contented people—reclining back as far as they wished, a TV in front of them, cozy slippers on their feet, a steak dinner on the way, and cheerful flight attendants doting over their every need.

"How much is the difference?" I daydreamed about the possibilities.

When the agent quoted the price I was snapped back to reality. I didn't have those kinds of resources! No wonder I flew economy—at least I could afford to buy my ticket on the spot. If I opted for first class, I'd have to plan ahead and save up well in advance.

When it came to the friendly skies, I'd spent my life opting for the quicker, cheaper alternative, flying economy class. Unfortunately, the same was true in relationships...only with more long-term regrets. Now I wished for something better. After a failed marriage of thirteen years and a myriad of dating relationships gone bad (before and after the marriage), I wondered if it was too late for me to upgrade. Was my romantic life beyond repair? Should I settle for the first tolerable guy that would have me? Had my only chance for a first class romance made a takeoff without me? With my limited resources, the prospects didn't look good.

The Problem: Doubt & Disbelief

Before we jump into my story, I need to share some important foundational problems in my thinking at this time—problems that led to my upgrade obstacles.

The limited resources keeping me out of something better were in the form of distorted thought patterns that resulted in my doubt and distrust of God:

My dating life is insignificant to God.
My future is left to chance.
God isn't big enough to help me solve my problems.

These kinds of thoughts left me insecure and fearful about turning over the ticketing controls to the One who said a seat could be secured for me up in front. I also believed additional lies that left me hopeless:

I've made so many mistakes that I don't deserve better.
It's too late for me.
I'm ruined.

Where did these lies come from? There's a verse in the Bible that says, "[Satan] was a murderer from the beginning, not holding to the truth, for there is no truth in him. When he lies, he speaks his native language, for he is a liar and the father of lies" (John 8:44). The original word for "satan" simply means adversary (not a name), which doesn't necessarily or always mean a nefarious being with horns and a pitchfork. Even God (and others) was described as a "satan" in the Old Testament when he opposed someone (Num. 22:22, 32). It can be anything or anyone that sabotages your progress, your happiness, your purpose, and your relationship to God, including other people, your negative or unhealthy thoughts, your bad habits, and even your conscious or unconscious baggage from the past.

I didn't exactly understand at that time that many "satans" had been working overtime in my life to steal, kill, and destroy (John 10:10) my Loving Father's best, abundant plans for my

The Table of Hope

life, by fueling me up with as many lies as possible. Hey, as long as they kept working, why not?

Since the days of old, many adversarial forces have been murdering our perception of God's character and His plans of good for us. Eve could certainly attest to this! In Genesis 3:4 a certain slithery, charming voice suggested to her that God gave her everything but that one "better" thing. God supposedly held out on her! So you see, through lies, Eve's innocent trust in the true character of her God was slowly being murdered.

Just like Eve, I'd "bitten into" the same lies. To aid this methodical character assassination against God, my adversarial thoughts pointed to certain circumstances and events from my past to persuade me that God didn't "come through" for me either, and that it was up to me singlehandedly to solve my own problems. Like repeated physical and emotional abuse I endured as a child, and consistent rejection from prominent men throughout my life. There was also the attempted sexual abuse from a longtime, trusted spiritual mentor (who was also a father figure) in 8th grade. Countless other disappointments and hardships added up over the years, and now this—a shattered heart and marriage. All I had worked for toward my own dreams lay in a heap of ashes, save my two resulting precious daughters.

With the backdrop of these seeming failures and disappointments, it wasn't that difficult to buy into beliefs that God either wasn't paying attention, or He was too busy with more important things. My perception of God's goodness was being challenged so deeply within me that I couldn't even find the words to verbalize the depth of my doubts and fears.

What next? Was solving my own problems or taking matters into my own hands the answer? Wasn't that ultimately how I got into this mess in the first place? Was asking God for help even a possibility for me in light of my trust issues and fiercely independent nature? As my Mom always liked to point out, I was one of those kids who had to figure things out for herself. I always thought I knew what was best for me without wanting much input.

The Perfect Fit

Planning and pursuing my own way ended up about as successful as a presidential deficit reduction plan. Was there a better way—something untried and true? Was there a way out of dreaded economy class?

The Solution: Insight

What I've learned along the way is that the only power these adversarial forces (dark thoughts, fears, shame) have over the lives of God's children are the lies we believe as a result of their delusions. That's it. But until we become aware of them and figure out what to do with them, they most often work.

So how do we overcome the false voices in our heads that get us stuck in patterns of unhappy choices? These unhealthy (often unconscious) patterns steal our mental health and ultimately happy lives and futures? What is going to give us that edge to let go of our doubt and start believing God? Maybe you're like me and you are good and ready for a new start in your life, but what will pull us through this time when crushing doubts beckon us to revert to what we've always known—settling for the wrong thing out of fear, impatience, or stubbornness? Unless we learn to recognize these downward spiraling patterns and replace them with transformative truths, an upgrade to fuzzy slippers and marinated rib eye is not going to happen.

Identifying and practicing truths, even in the face of doubt, are one sure method of moving us beyond the veil of economy, but how do we identify them in a meaningful way that will encourage us to change our choices and experiences? I'm going to walk you through some tangible examples from my personal story to give you some inspiration.

Little did I know there was a catch 22 involved in my relearning the character of God by experience. It all started with that one little practice that's easy to pronounce, but so difficult to act upon. Without it, there can be no intimate learning of the character of God from the inside out.

The Table of Hope

The Vehicle: Faith

Faith is putting belief and hope into action. It's the difference between saying you believe that the rather thin looking ice is strong enough to hold you up, and actually stepping out onto the ice to prove it. By definition, situations requiring faith never look sturdy, safe, or even wise to the untrained eye.

I've found that God is eagerly waiting to prove Himself to us when we risk belief. God's commitment to our becoming process, no matter how thin in appearance, can be relied upon to hold us up when we put all our weight on it. But much like a bungy cord is useless around your ankles until you take the plunge, God's plan and power is useless in your life unless you believe it and try it for yourself.

Faith is developed two ways: primarily (and necessarily) through our own experiential leaps into the uncertainty of God's leading, and also through hearing about the experiences of others doing the same. For instance, even though King David had an amazing relationship with God, he also had many difficult things happen to him in his life—many of them beyond his control. If anyone tested out the promises of God, it was David. What did he discover and believe about God's character? "Taste and see that the Lord is good. Oh, the joys of those who trust in Him! Those who trust in the Lord will *never lack any good thing*" (Psalm 34). David is a man who knew! He had tried and tested God's promises repeatedly.

Still, I had significant doubts. I did want peace and a hopeful future, but I didn't want boredom. Would the plans God intended for my life (marriage or not) be too placid and uneventful for me? Sometimes I envisioned His call upon my life as rounding up used tea bags for the missionaries in Africa, or maybe opening a daycare. I feared God would require the very thing that would leave me the least fulfilled or happy in light of my personality and desires. I sincerely hoped that God's way would truly be better than anything I could do for myself—a real adventure as enchanting as David's life.

Delving into Samuel and Kings, I saw how David's desire for God's leading brought about such an exciting life full of surprises. Even when it didn't look to David like anything significant was happening on the surface, a grand, unfolding plan was in the works.

We are so fortunate to get the historical overview because we get to see both David's part and God's part—the part that David couldn't see. God shaped events by placing people and circumstances in the right places at the right time to fulfill His promises to David and to work out a plan for good in his life. Although it took David many years to see conflict resolution and fulfillment of promises, we have the benefit of seeing all those years being compressed down into a few hours of reading.

God doesn't play favorites, so I figured if God orchestrated such an adventure for David; He would do it for anyone who asked. When David trusted God and didn't lose heart, even after years of waiting, God fulfilled all His good plans. I wanted that special adventure and romance with God in my life, even if it took years. For once, I wanted to see things turn out God's way—in God-sized, breath-taking events, not the simple, average, problematic, dead-end things I could do (and had done so far) for myself.

If David had so many difficult things happen during his lifetime that were out of his control, and he could still say he didn't lack any good thing, perhaps what I lacked was a right perspective about my circumstances. Those who wronged me were not a reflection on God's character, but were still within the sovereign power of God's ultimate plan of good (Gen. 50:20). I also had to admit that many of my problems—including the consequences from my marriage and divorce—were the result of many of my own choices.

> I remember my affliction and my wandering, the bitterness and the gall. I well remember them, and my soul is downcast within me. Yet this I call to mind and therefore I have hope: Because of the Lord's great love we are not consumed. His mercies are new every morning..." (Lamentation 3:19-22).

The Table of Hope

So what was my decision going to be? I stood with great uncertainty on the bridge, bungy cord around my ankles, teetering on the brink of trust. Was I going to keep trying my own devices and solutions that had only brought me pain and emptiness, or was I going to take a risk and trust God with my future? I wanted to take a chance of experiencing fulfilled promises—promises like "a crown of beauty for ashes, the oil of gladness instead of mourning, and a garment of praise instead of a spirit of despair (Isaiah 61:3)." I understood those promises didn't necessarily mean I would ever remarry, but they surely sounded like first class to me.

Making a Connection

Have you ever seen one of those blindfolded kids at a birthday party, trying to hit a piñata with a skinny stick? While blindfolded, someone spins her around into dizzy oblivion, and then they turn her loose to locate the prize. It is so frustrating watching that stick swing around, usually not even in the direction of the target. You sure don't want to get between that kid and her candy. She is so intent on making contact; people have to run for their lives just to stay out of the way.

I felt like that kid—dizzy from lies, unable to see a thing that God was doing around me. But then I swung the stick around frantically in the dark, trying to land on God's promises. I knew I had to keep going no matter how much I missed, because at some point I would make a connection if I didn't give up. And then, when I least expected it, I finally made a hit—I found the prized assurance that I would be rewarded for my faith.

I can just imagine God watching us, rooting us on the whole time, thrilled when our stick finally hits the target. Secretly, I know that He nudged my stick in the right direction; it's no less than I would have done for my own kids. Of course I wasn't expecting a hit at someone else's wedding, of all places! God loves to be unpredictable and surprising at times. Anyhow, I think I hear music. We can't be late for this wedding. Something amazing is about to happen.

The Perfect Fit

Watch for ~~Road~~ Rose Signs
(Dream God's Dreams for Your Life)

Before arriving at the wedding, we have to make an unusual detour—through a graveyard. This particular graveyard is located in the book of Ezekiel. EZ's book is a little like reading an account by a man on a mushroom trip, which just might have been the case. In chapter 37, God took Ezekiel down to a valley of old, dried up bones. The bones were apparently human bones, left over from one of many battles. Ezekiel stood there looking around, wondering why God brought him to such a place, consumed by death and defeat.

Suddenly a voice from this graveyard proclaimed, "Our bones are dried up and our hope is gone." Then God told Ezekiel to prophesy to the bones to come back to life. As EZ obeyed, calling the bones together, they made an unforgettable clattering and rattling, rising up to attach in all the right places. They became flesh right in front of his eyes! Then God breathed His breath of life into them so that they were restored.

I'm pretty sure the intended point of this passage is that the hopes and dreams of the people Israel were a heap of dried up bones in the graveyard, just like mine and maybe, just like yours. God is now and has always been in the business of giving and reviving dreams. He looks at the pieces lying around in our valleys of death and destruction, visualizing how He wants to bring new life and new dreams for us.

Because of the ways God began working in my life and filling me with hope at this time, I could practically feel the comforting breeze of His breath stirring a new dream for me.

The Sign

The setting was a beautiful candlelight wedding of one of my co-workers on a festive December evening. Around that time I'd been praying fervently that God would send me a sign of hope about my future. I deeply desired another chance for a God-centered marriage and a healthy father figure for my young girls. All my life I had dreamed of this kind of family. After all,

The Table of Hope

wasn't it God who said, "It is not good for the man (or woman!) to be alone" (Genesis 2:18)? Especially as a mother, I didn't feel the particular call of single parenting on my life. The hope for a like-hearted mate seemed like a reasonable request.

After the wedding ceremony, the time came for that traditional [silly?], superstitious practice where the bride throws her bouquet to the throngs of pining, desperate gals, promising the one who catches it to be the next bride. I may have been desperate, but I'm certainly not superstitious. Although my friends were trying to push me toward the expectant group of women, I purposely stepped back at least fifteen feet from the group, blending back into the crowd of onlookers.

Looking around the room at the lavish Christmas decorations, trying to appear disinterested, I nearly missed my own commotion. As the bride threw the bouquet, I caught the bizarre unfolding of events out of the corner of my eye. Several girls jumped up to catch the bouquet at the same time, much like a jump ball at center court in a basketball game—and about as graceful, too! As they did, the bouquet was jolted back up into the air a second time. A single white rose tore away from the rest of the flowers, flew in a high arc away from the crowd, and landed perfectly right side up into my clasped hands. The crowd let out a few gasps of surprise about the amazing chain of events, and a few even asked me, over chuckles, how it happened. Unfortunately, this was just before the days of everyone capturing every event on cell phone cameras.

Was it chance? Was it a strange coincidence? I didn't think so. It seemed too precise and too intentional to be an accident. Because of the context of the bridal bouquet and wedding, I highly suspected it was God's humorous plot of reassurance that He can even use superstition if desired to announce His plans. In this case, presumably bringing a marriage partner into my life again. But I had to be careful not to be too presumptuous. His plans are never defined or constructed by my own ideals or imaginations. I would just have to watch and wait for whatever would materialize in His way and His time, but it was sure to be special!

The Perfect Fit

With this new clue about my future promise, I could hardly stand the suspense. How could God possibly expect someone like me—someone with the patience of a New York City taxi driver—not to take matters into my own hands? I had the clear feeling that if I weren't careful, I would miss out on something extraordinary.

I sincerely asked God that day to help me not miss His divine leading with ignorance or impatience. If the white rose did mean that He was going to bless me with a certain husband of His choice, I wanted clear road signs—even if He had to paste them to my eyelids!

God, I believe You are telling me You have a special man picked out for my future. I am seriously going to need Your help to be patient and discerning! When the time comes and You bring him into my life, please, give me a sign by having him present me with a white rose, so I will know it's Your leading.

I had heard of similar requests answered for others, so it didn't seem unreasonable. After all, I was asking God for help and direction regarding my future. What Loving Parent wouldn't grant such a simple plea for help? What Fair Judge wouldn't grant such a favorable ruling? In my best attorney impersonation, I approached the bench.

[Clears throat] Didn't You say yourself, "If any of you lacks wisdom, he should ask God, who gives generously to all without finding fault, and it will be given to him" (James 1:5)? Didn't You also say in Proverbs 3:6, "In all your ways submit to him and he will make your paths straight"?

Believing God would answer my request, I took an oath of silence never to tell anyone about the white rose request until my future promise was fulfilled. It was a little secret between God and me, and I could only imagine that it was going to be both exciting and difficult to keep.

The Instruction

As much as the Israelites are criticized for their fickle nature, constant doubt, infuriating impatience, and blatant disobedience when they left Egypt, they looked like devoted and

The Table of Hope

unwavering followers compared to me. Not long after the rose incident, the hope and excitement wearing off, I began struggling with trust again.

So God, when You say this thing about "a thousand years is like a day..." that kind of resonates. I've only got a few years to work with here. What good will it do if I'm using social security and Depends® before You make good on Your promise?

Patience and delayed gratification for the sake of something better seemed like unreachable goals for someone like me. Still, I saved the rose in a visible place in my kitchen to remind me often of God's mystery promise to me. Who knew—perhaps a visible reminder would help me wait patiently and calmly for God's promises, much like the daily manna and quail helped the Israelites do the same [ya, right!].

Have you ever tried to pretend that you can't (or didn't) hear God? This usually happens to me when I want to do my own thing or want to get away with something that I know is wrong. Well, not long after I prayed to God for direction, He answered. He started by giving instructions tailored to my individual set of circumstances—instructions that were so clear they couldn't have been more obvious than a road map with only one highway. Coming to me at least four different times through different mediums was this directive: *"Stay out of relationships until your ex-husband either remarries or comes back for reconciliation."* This was one of those times when I knew that if I chose to do my own thing, I couldn't blame Him later when things got really messy or miserable.

It's important for you to know that I believe God works differently with different situations and people. This was the direction He gave me at the time because of many extenuating circumstances—I wasn't enduring physical abuse, both my husband and I had been unfaithful toward the end of our marriage and equally bore fault in violating our marriage vows, and most important was that our children did not deserve the loss of their sufficiently functional biological family. They had two highly engaged, loving parents who, together, could provide the stable home environment they needed to thrive. I believe in

The Perfect Fit

most cases, divorce is not the best answer, especially when kids are involved. However, I have learned with age and life experience that each person must listen to God and their hearts to decide, because there is no one-size-fits-all. Thankfully, God works in our lives individually for our highest and best spiritual growing process, which is why the black and white approach of many churches must be thoughtfully questioned.

In my case God showed me that, even though my husband had divorced me, He wanted me to demonstrate an attitude of reconciliation with single-heartedness until that door was firmly shut.

How did I hear God's direction on the matter? The first came as a recognized conviction of the Spirit—quiet as a summer breeze but impactful as a locomotive. Through my prayers, God impressed heavily upon me to stay single in heart and action until further notice. The second came through counseling with my pastor who urged me, in light of the circumstances of our separation, to honor my marriage vows "till death do us part." He suggested that if my ex-husband married someone else, our vows would be "put to death," and then I would be free to remarry. The third came through my sister and her husband, who knew my situation intimately, and confirmed through their insider's perspectives and love for me that I should not seek out other relationships until there was no hope for reviving my marriage.

God has rarely, if ever, affirmed something four times. But one Sunday I visited a church that I had never attended before. At the end of the service, the pastor invited anyone needing prayer to come forward. I was having one of my dark days and was desperate for spiritual support, so I felt compelled to go forward. I don't even recall being able to ask for prayer because the tears were flowing so freely when I went forward that I couldn't speak. This pastor, who didn't know anything about me, spoke several affirmations to me that exactly paralleled the things God had spoken to me privately.

"God has collected all your tears. He will give you great joy in proportion to your former sorrow. He has a wonderful plan for

The Table of Hope

your life, but right now He wants your *undivided heart*. He wants you to focus completely upon Him with patience and obedience. Wait for Him. He will prepare you and restore to you all the years that the locusts have eaten. He will use your life to minister peace and hope to others who are hurting..."

Moments like that are what you call spiritual CPR. They're like that great first gasp of air when you break the surface of the water after holding your breath as long as possible. But along with the comforting affirmation often comes sobering responsibility.

In the midst of the message, God gently admonished me to drop my fears of being alone and not to look for the attention or approval of any man—one of my deeply rooted compulsions originating in my youth. *He* wanted to be the First Love of my life, and He assured me that He would be everything I needed.

"For it was I, the LORD your God, who rescued you from the land of Egypt. Open your mouth wide, and I will fill it with good things...put your trust in Me and you will never be disappointed." (Ps. 81:10, 22:5).

He wanted the chance to heal my broken heart by filling me up with His unfailing love and incredible healing touch, something that could only take place if I focused on Him completely for a season. This would surely not happen if I poured out my dwindling emotional energy on men and relationships.

The Stumble

I wish I could say that after all the assurances—the white rose, the pastor, and the others—that I perfectly trusted and waited God with the patience of Mother Teresa. But as I said, patience isn't one of my strong points. Although I did verbalize a commitment to my ex-husband that I wouldn't consider remarriage unless he remarried first in order to allow for possible reconciliation, the verbal commitment was only lip service to God's directive. My impending actions would prove my full compliance—or not.

The Perfect Fit

Living each day was the hard part. I had too much time on my hands to think about how long it was taking and how things would move along more quickly if I helped them along. I started rationalizing that since my ex-husband was in a relationship, why couldn't I be in one, too? Then self-pity chimed in his two cents, "Poor you. Everyone else is out having fun and getting what they want while you're here all by yourself. That's so not fair!"

More rationalizations headed in while the door was open. Just because I might get into a relationship, doesn't mean it would have to be serious or lead to anything long-term. If I were to, say, find a man who would just be a good friend, it would solve my immediate loneliness problem. It would be fun. Besides, it works in the movies!

My great rationalizing abilities rivaled that of a modern day presidential cabinet. They quite possibly started years earlier on the way to the cookie jar. I have a great fondness for cookies and I will sneak them at any opportunity. If I even start thinking about the cookie jar, I'm already doomed. In the same way, starting to chew on old self-soothing patterns of getting attention from men was about to sabotage my best intentions.

Not more than three months after the powerful assurances and direction by God for me to be single-hearted for Him, a tick came out from the long winter, looking for a dog. Let's face it. I didn't feel complete without the presence and assurance of a man in my life. Sure, I had improved somewhat since the days of moral failure and seeing where this unhealthy need for attention led, but I still couldn't connect my heart with the notion that God alone was enough, or that I didn't need a man to be happy.

The Internet seemed like a rather harmless alternative to dating. It was more or less like making new friends—not dating—for Pete's sake! And the men I met online were Christian men, no less. Not unlike eating a dozen fat-free chocolate chip cookies so I didn't ruin my diet. It couldn't hurt to make "friends" via the Internet. Besides, it might come in handy for "later," since the only eligible males I had met so far

The Table of Hope

in the sparsely populated state of Wyoming were sheep. Any men I met were all going to be long distance anyhow—what harm could befall? It might be helpful to note that this was in the early stages of Internet dating when it was very new, desperate, and creepy. Everyone then believed that it for losers and was surely a recipe for getting oneself murdered. For that reason, it was not something you readily admitted to anyone!

It wasn't too difficult to find another needy soul—another tick looking for a dog. "Matt" and I met on a Christian singles site, which at least sounded more admirable. It's interesting how the mind and will make alliances to trick one into getting ahead of the plan. Soon enough, I'd made my way close enough to the cookie jar until I believed it was okay to get into a relationship with a "Christian man." *There's no harm done as long as he's a believer...maybe there's a man on here that God wants me to be with down the road and I'll miss out on meeting him if I don't try now...God isn't hung up on a little timing problem. Quit being such a martyr.*

Despite my crafty rationalizations, I knew what God had told me to do. As a result, I constantly felt guilty while pursuing this relationship. Whatever emotional energy I possessed going into it was dried up like the soil in August. The truth is that God's hand was heavy upon me, not to *keep me from* something, but to *save me for something much* better. God was practically saying, *"Hey bozo, I already told you I have something wonderful for you, and this isn't it! You've gotten way ahead of me again."*

The Conviction

How does God continue to have patience with a dense, impatient, and rebellious children who doubt His absolute desire for and commitment to our happiness? He won't ever make us obey, but He will certainly apply pressure at times when necessary to promote our well being and safety. Most importantly, He wants us to obey because we *want* to obey. He wants our motives to be love fueled by gratitude for all of the kindness and mercy that continually shows us, because in the long run, love is much more motivating than fear, guilt, or coercion.

But many times God has to "let out the leash" and give us over to our independent, stubborn inclinations in order to help us come face to face with our misperceptions and refine our motives in our relationships with Him. Leashes are normally for dogs because, by nature, most dogs are willful and naïve.

God had to give a little yank on my leash when I started to get a little too far out into old, dream-threatening territory. I'll never forget the day I was on my way to see Matt for a visit. There I was, sitting in an airport, trying to kill some time with one of my favorite books, a brilliant allegory by Hannah Hurnard, *Hinds Feet on High Places*. As I began reading, God began speaking to me through the book so directly and so loudly, it was as if I was being paged over the airport intercom system.

"Julie...this is God speaking. There's no need to pick up a yellow paging telephone. I can talk to you right where you are sitting..."

Don't Settle for a Skunk
(Good Enough is Not Enough)

Feeling rather exposed, I looked around to see if anyone else noticed anything out of the usual. Well, at least no one was staring at me. As my eyes fell back onto the page, I got that familiar feeling closing around my neck, "YANK!" The leash pulled tight as I read these words:

> "I think," said the Shepherd (Jesus) gently, "that lately the way seemed a little easier and the sun shone, and you came to a place where you could rest. You forgot for a while that you were my little handmaiden, 'Acceptance-with-Joy,' and were beginning to tell yourself it really was time that I led you back to the mountains (the promised destination) and up to the High Places. When you wear the weed of impatience in

> your heart instead of the flower Acceptance-with-Joy, you will always find your enemies get an advantage over you."
>
> Much Afraid blushed. She knew how right he was in his diagnosis. It had been easier to accept the hard path and to be patient when the sea was gray and dull than now when the sun shone and everything else around looked bright and happy and satisfied. She put her hand in the Shepherd's and said sorrowfully, "You are quite right. I have been thinking that you are allowing me to follow this path too long and that you were forgetting your promise." Then she added, looking steadfastly into his face, "But I do tell you now with all my heart that you are my Shepherd whose voice I love to hear and obey, and that it is my joy to follow you. You choose, my Lord, and I will obey."
>
> The Shepherd stooped down and picked up a stone, which was lying beside her feet and said smilingly, "Put this in your bag with the other stones as a memorial of this day...of your promise that you will wait patiently until I give you your heart's desire."[1]

Feeling a sudden sense of shame wash over me, accompanied by the sensation of lead weights attached to every limb, I slammed the book shut. Busted! I was not ready to echo Much Afraid's words of obedience, but conscience-stricken just the same. I knew without a doubt that God was speaking to me through that passage, exposing my weed of impatience.

This is a sure way to put a damper on my trip before it starts, and it's the last time I open that book while I'm exploring the boundaries of my leash, I thought with disgust. Unfortunately, trying to arrange my own future was about to make my life much more complicated.

Crash and Burn

Contrary to certain warped perceptions (and beliefs), asserting our idea of freedom is not usually very free. On the contrary, inviting God's leading and assistance, we find He's not the rigid taskmaster our minds would have us believe. The

The Perfect Fit

exact opposite is true! The more we invite God's leading into our lives, the more freedom and peace we experience. In John 8:34-36, "Jesus replied, 'I tell you the truth, everyone who sins is a slave to sin. Now a slave has no permanent place in the family, but a son belongs to it forever. So if the Son sets you free, you will be free indeed.'"

I love that verse because it points out that we are no longer slaves or even servants of God. We are sons and daughters welcomed into the Family, if only we would believe it. The more we try to run our own lives, the more separated from our Source and enslaved we feel. The more we consciously choose the will of Christ and our connectedness to Source, the more we are set free. What an exciting paradox.

Barging down my familiar path as a slave, God still continued pointing my way to connection and freedom—even to the point of trying to reach me boldly while I was enroute to disobedience.

It's no surprise that, since I had rationalized everything about this relationship from the beginning, I was about to be greatly disillusioned. On this trip to see Matt, it became glaringly apparent that his faith was all talk and no action. In the short time we were together, I got sucked in to his compromising arguments, despite my decision to save myself for my future husband.

"We have both been married already. It won't hurt if we sleep together. Besides, God doesn't expect us to be perfect."

"Sure, God doesn't expect us to be perfect, but He still wants us to protect our hearts. If we love Him and ourselves, we recognize those values are for our own good. I don't think it's right to rush into a sexual relationship this soon."

"So then let's get married!"

"Are you kidding? We've only known each other for a couple months!"

"Look," he said, his tone changing to condescendingly sweet. "You are way too legalistic. You make a mistake and beat yourself up about it. Yes, we try to have some self-control, but God doesn't get all bent out of shape if we mess up. He knows

The Table of Hope

we can't be perfect. *He doesn't even expect it!* Don't you think He understands that we have certain needs? I don't think He's watching our every move waiting to punish us over every little mistake like you seem to think. My God offers more grace than that. You're way too guilt-ridden."

Matt's rationalizations made me angry, but also planted some seeds of doubt. Could I really be that legalistic? Didn't God still want us to try to protect and preserve ourselves even though we'd both been married before? Matt did seem to want to live for God in many ways. Was I too idealistic at my age in hoping to find a man who had the same values? Now that I thought about it, I hadn't met very many Christian men in my lifetime that lived any different than any other men when it came to sexual purity. Maybe I expected too much.

Listening to his arguments, I allowed Matt to sway my thinking. Confusing thoughts made my convictions fuzzy, and I compromised my desires and goals to save myself for sexual intimacy. I was temporarily convinced that the guy who waits until he's married to have sex doesn't exist in this day and age.

Afterward, I felt like a hot air balloon that had just been deflated. Where a short time before I'd been floating peacefully on the heights doing things God's way, soon after I was plunged into a deep valley of regret and gloom.

The Counterfeit

Until the point where I actually gave in to sex, I waffled about my relationship with Matt. Yes, deep down I had many moments when I felt convicted, or when I lacked peace. But because of my inexperience with these situations and the power of delusion, I had several unexplained coincidences that made it seem as if God might actually be leading me into a relationship with Matt. My straying off the path was much more identifiable in hindsight than it was in the moment because I was impatient, confused, and vulnerable. This ultimately meant that I was getting sidetracked and delayed from experiencing God's best plan for me.

The Perfect Fit

Counterfeits deceive us into accepting something that looks like the real thing (or the good enough thing), but isn't. This sobering and frightening realization left me wondering how I, someone well versed in being duped, was going to have the discernment or confidence to recognize the real thing?

My question led me to consider the well known practice for counterfeit identification procedures. A currency counterfeit specialist first learns to identify phony currency by studying—very, very carefully—*authentic* currency. He has to have a standard, something true and right to compare to, so that's why he only studies the real thing. Then, when a counterfeit dollar passes in front of him, it just doesn't look or feel right. There is something about the texture, the color, and the overall appearance of it that isn't right, because he is accustomed to the feel of what is authentic moving across his fingers and gaze.

Our lives have to follow this example if we are ever going to recognize the truth and not be swayed and confused by every seemingly good thing that comes along, especially when it comes to relationships. If you want to know what an authentic "God's best" relationship looks like, you have to study authentic God-centered relationships, which is what you are doing right now by reading this book.

Of course, the Bible offers many inspiring examples and principles that apply to character and relationships. There are also inspiring books and accounts of people who elaborate about what God's best looked like in their lives as well. Getting to know and spend time with such couples in person is even better! Even though the events of their stories will all be unique, the foundational elements and outcomes will all be the similar.

Because we can easily be lured into old unhealthy patterns, we need to expose ourselves to as much authenticity as possible so we won't be fooled with confusing counterfeits. These often appear alluring, which means they don't necessarily show up with claws and fangs. On the contrary, they trick us into falling for something that appears to be a "good enough" thing, but is only a fraudulent imitation that prevents the best thing for us.

The Table of Hope

My encounter with Matt left me emptier than before, and it wasn't long before my restlessness and lack of peace drove me back to longing. I missed the joy of feeling an uninhibited, sweet connection to God. It felt as though God was as distant as the stars and disapprovingly cut off of me, which caused unnecessary suffering.

I have since become wiser in my relationship with God to know that it is impossible to cut off fellowship with God or to garner His disproval. Those feelings were only based in misperception and misinformation, often learned from misguided teachers and preachers. God is never distant or disapproving, the realization of which brings great relief and even more positive motives for obedience. I might miss something amazing through my impatience, but my relationship with God was never in jeopardy, never distant. However, the price of not trusting God and not waiting for His promises weren't worth any short-lived pleasures—and surely not this miserable relationship of my own doing.

Finally, that very weekend, I got the courage to end the relationship—a decision that was really hurtful to Matt. I felt guilty for causing him unnecessary pain since I had wrongly entered into the relationship to begin with. That is another consequence of taking matters into our own hands—not only do we hurt ourselves, we also hurt others in the process. Thankfully, when I approached God with a repentant heart, I was strengthened and encouraged, filled with that mysterious and permeating peace through my younger self perceptions of restored relationship with Him.

Let's Make Another Deal

I'd like to say that from this point forward, I perfectly trusted God, waiting on Him with more deeply resolved patience. I had absolutely no excuse not to trust God after all He had done to give me assurance, forgiveness, and second chances. I had seen once again the fallout that came into my life as a result of not trusting Him. Oh, how I wish this part of my story didn't have to be so repetitious. It's hard recognizing internalized lies for their fruit—they *always promise much more than they deliver.* But you would think I would be smarter than the dog by now.

There's a saying that "old habits die hard," but many old habits are really just old lies that keep recycling as long as they keep working. We're never told up front that there will be consequences like guilt, shame, emptiness, grief, anxiety, and even more problems to solve than before.

So, once again, about three months later, unwilling to be patient and accept being alone, I began searching looking for another leash. I started a relationship with "Tom"—another poor, unsuspecting victim. Somehow I believed this time it would be different, and that we would most definitely "just be friends." Besides, I did more to check out the spiritual commitment of this new Internet acquaintance. I called his pastor for an extensive interview, even before we met. I covered all the bases. God could just sit back and rest easy because I'd done my homework. He wouldn't even have to be bothered this time—I had everything under control!

From a worldly standpoint, Tom was a great catch! He was boo-koo loaded (a.k.a. rich!) and I found myself wondering if money really could buy happiness. My longing heart loomed on the scene with the latest array of alluring selections, just like Monte Hall on the long ago game show, "Let's Make a Deal," offering me all three doors *and* the bag.

"Yes, Julie, all these can be yours just for the asking…

"DOOR #1: a *huge* lake home in the mountains;

"DOOR #2: a red mustang convertible—I know you've always wanted one; and…

"DOOR #3: frequent world travel—your favorite pastime. Anything else you want is already in the bag. What's it going to be, Julie?"

Uh…uh…so tempting!

The lifestyle he offered was so mesmerizing, that I actually began hoping Tom would be the one to give me the awaited white rose. I asked God about it, forgetting that I was the one who initiated the relationship, not Him.

The Table of Hope

Surely this guy with the money and the fabulous lifestyle (oh yeah...and a genuine faith) will be "the one," right God? Didn't you say something about blessing your children?

Tom did send me flowers—sometimes two or three bouquets a week. Each time, I received them expectantly, practically dumping the whole lot out on the counter, looking over, under and through the flowers for that white rose. There were purple chrysanthemums, pink carnations, white daisies, orange tiger lilies, yellow roses, red roses, pink roses—you get the idea—and one pathetically desperate woman with bits and pieces of flowers strewn all over her kitchen. But no white roses.

Hey God, we talked about "white roses." Did you forget?

It wasn't long before my house resembled a funeral home and the bi-weekly flower arrangements started wearing out their welcome. This flower thing wasn't fitting into my fantasy ideals of the unique moment that I would receive a white rose—you know, the moment like in the movies where I'm standing barefoot in a flowing white gauze dress fluttering lightly in the wind, surrounded by a field of daisies. Suddenly a brave warrior charges in on his gallant steed, white rose in hand. Tenderly he reaches down and places the rose in my outstretched hand, and we ride off into the sunset on the way to our romantic destiny. Oh yes, and music is playing in the background.

I imagined countless ways I might receive a rose. But each time I wondered how God could possibly pull it off, since He would undoubtedly (and hopefully) do something I couldn't even imagine. What if I'd already thought of every possible scenario? Judging from the above scene, I know you are thinking that I'm setting myself up for some grave disappointment (or a well-deserved trip to my psychiatrist).

Skunked Again

My ex-husband scheduled his remarriage a few months later, so I figured Tom and I could start out as friends and maybe reevaluate the possibilities in a few months. As you could probably tell by the floral shop in my home, Tom had other plans. He wasn't feeling too *friendly*, if you know what I mean.

The Perfect Fit

In practically just minutes, Tom's feelings for me grew like a bamboo shoot. His ultra-smothering behavior left me feeling like the object of Pepe Le Pew's affections in the famous cartoon, where he's obsessed with a poor cat that looks like she would rather eat rat poison than endure his aggressive courtship strategies. Three words often came to mind: smothered, cornered, and repulsed. *Yank! Yank!* Oh, yes, and strangled.

The weekend he drove down to visit me at my parent's home—against my wishes—I was an emotional wreck! My Mom was at her wits' end. Every time she saw me come into the room after talking to Tom, she handed me another Kleenex for my tear-streaked, blotchy face. I single-handedly emptied every box of Kleenex in the house that weekend.

My Dad, on the other hand, was developing strong feelings for Tom. They shared a common passion for hunting and fishing, a prerequisite for welcoming any potential son-in-law into the inner circle. They sat around the breakfast table, long after everyone else had tired of hearing about the latest conquest, discussing every hunting and fishing topic available—from gun cleaning products and the best walleye fishing spots, to proper elk gutting techniques.

"Care for another elk sausage, Julie?" Tom asked with his mouth full as I cleared the dishes.

"No! Thanks."

Tom was so pushy that, during this weekend together—and only a few weeks into the supposed "friendship,"—he was already talking marriage—with my parents, right in front of me, as if I was on board! He started the conversation in their wood paneled living room, sitting forward on the cream-colored leather sofa.

"Sam and Molly, I want to let you know what my plans are. I think I would make a great husband for Julie. I certainly have a lot to offer her." He looked as if he might flex his biceps at any moment to prove it.

"Undoubtedly." My Dad beamed back his total agreement, thinking of all the future hunting excursions. The angry darts I shot at him across the room with my eyes went unnoticed.

The Table of Hope

"Anyhow, I love Julie, and I'd like to marry her. I will take good care of her and provide well for her."

Cough, cough! He loves me? He doesn't even know me! It was all I could do not to throw myself onto the floor and start a full-blown tantrum.

Dad was all thumbs up, beaming his approval. Mom, on the other hand, held true to her sensitive nature when she saw the look on my face. "Maybe we should take more time to think about this. You've only known each other a short time."

I wanted to raise my hand, *excuse me, I hate to intrude in your private conversation, but since this is my future too, could I have a say? I am not just another elk waiting to be shot for your trophy room. You don't win a woman the same way you hunt down an animal. You obviously don't even know what love is. My heart will never feel safe with you.*

Instead, unable to speak, I headed into the kitchen for a moment of solitude. Sitting down at the table, I felt so ashamed of myself. Here I was, about to hurt another poor guy who didn't even know what was going on inside of me, all because of my impatience. I was wrong for getting ahead of God and encouraging Tom's attention. And now, once again, I felt lonelier with Tom than I ever did without him. There was just one thing left to do.

I just wanted peace again.
I just wanted to be alone again.
I just wanted to get rid of the skunk.

I sent Tom down the road in his cute red Mustang convertible—the one thing I did love about him. I felt so relieved and lightened in spirit, even—happy. As the car disappeared from sight, however, my Dad cried his eyes out on my shoulder.

Good is Not Best

Either of these two men, Matt or Tom, could have easily fooled me into thinking they were the best God could do for me. Both men were professing Christians who claimed they had a committed relationship with God. They were each, from all appearances, a good catch—involved in church and ministry, nice looking, athletic, smart, and successful in business. There was no *good* reason to think they might not be potential life partners. But there was a *God* reason.

Just because a man loves God, and by all appearances perfectly suitable husband material, that does not make him God's best *for me* any more than a Santa suit makes a guy Santa Clause. Throughout my life and especially my relationships with men, I had typically been enticed by things that were by all appearances *good*, but those things kept me from pursuing *best*. *Even if I didn't buy into ruining my life with a bad choice, I could still miss a once in a lifetime opportunity by settling for "good enough."*

So what does God's best look like? How can we know beyond a doubt that we have found the real thing? Hopefully you have caught a few insights already, but let's keep going on this journey toward authentic love. I think there's a certain Road Runner who can give us some helpful advice.

Recharge the Road Runner
(TNT Self-Sabotage)

I love the movie, "What About Bob," where an obsessive-compulsive patient, Bob Wiley, starts receiving psychiatric treatment from a renowned psychiatrist, Dr. Leo Marvin. Using Dr. Marvin's book, "Baby Steps," Bob begins making small improvements and breakthroughs in recovering from his disorder. However, a lot of Bob's "improvements" come through unbelievably hilarious tactics of encroaching upon the psychiatrist's family and personal life (including a budding romantic interest between Bob and Dr. Marvin's sister). Eventually Leo, driven to manic desperation, resorts to one last attempt to get rid of Bob, under the guise of a supposed legitimate psychological treatment—"death therapy."

Dr. Marvin attaches a large amount of timed explosives to Bob's back, after tying him up securely in the dark forest at night. Ever the optimist, Bob perceives "death therapy" as a

The Table of Hope

legitimate intervention intended to help him. Cool headed and contemplative, he begins successfully untying himself, both literally and emotionally, while working through many of his fears and obsessions. Ultimately, Bob goes to Dr. Marvin's house to thank him for the cure, setting down the bundle of explosives on Dr. Marvin's doorstep, where it finally times out and detonates, blowing up the vacation lake house. At this point, Dr. Marvin has to be institutionalized.

At this point in my journey, I felt like Bob Wiley. Before I could experience my own special, healthy love story, it was absolutely necessary that I take "baby steps" down the path to my own version of "death therapy." An orchestrated death of my unhealthy patterns and self-sabotaging ways was the only promising answer for the chance of a better future. It is a pattern of this world that all fresh new life is preceded by a certain amount of dormancy and even death of the old that no longer serves the new.

Often mistaken as "moral failure," *sin* is actually the unpleasant consequences of our perception of separateness from God and each other. This perception drives us to engage in hurtful behaviors, rather than living in the joyful realization of Union with God and others, which is more in line with the ancient meaning of Scripture (before early Roman Catholicism with its obsession of moral piety). The perception of separation is the "thief," or that which robs us of the abundant life that Jesus spoke of (John 10:10). The end result is isolation from transformational Love and relationships. If you or I want to become a new person, we can learn to follow the example of Christ, walking in the way of trust, connection, and genuine love for ourselves and others. Then we find that God's plan for us, even though we don't often have the ability to recognize it at times, is for our best and highest!

Letting go of your (often too small) dreams and sacrificing that which doesn't serve you, especially when the dream is what you have lived your life for, is an agonizing process that no person can help you through. It is a place you have to go—

The Perfect Fit

alone—with God. In *My Utmost for His Highest,* Oswald Chambers calls this a "white funeral."

> No one experiences complete sanctification (being set apart or fully in tune with God) without going through a "white funeral"—the burial of the old life. If there has never been this crucial moment of change through death, sanctification will never be more than an elusive dream. There must be a "white funeral," a death with only one resurrection—a resurrection [now] into the life of Jesus Christ. Have you really come to your last days? You have often come to them in your mind, but have you really experienced them? You cannot die or go to your funeral in a mood of excitement. Death means you stop being. ...Is there a place in your life to which you go back in memory with humility and overwhelming gratitude, so that you can honestly proclaim, "Yes, it was then, at my white funeral, that I made an agreement with God."[2]

Funeral is a good word for it—there is nothing easy or cheerful about annihilating the destructive illusion that you are independent, or separate, or worthless, undeserving, or...? (Add your own self-sabotaging obstacles).

Remember the cartoon "Road Runner?" It's one of those cartoons that, if you've seen one episode, you've seen them all: Wile E. Coyote, hopelessly obsessed with destroying the Road Runner, stops at nothing to achieve his goal.

Because of Coyote's relentless pursuit, the Road Runner is constantly on the alert for his archenemy. Although Coyote looks pitifully sweet and innocent, his ambition is ever the same. Every day, he plots tricky and drastic measures to ambush his victim—TNT, poison, boulders the size of houses, false roads that drop off cliffs—all to be finished with the bird.

Why do you think the Coyote is so intent upon the demise of his harmless and innocent victim? Let me suggest that, like our mental obstacles, Wile can't stand to lose. His insane determination to destroy the bird and win the battle comes at any personal cost.

The Table of Hope

But Coyote is no match for Road Runner. Ever aware of the crafty schemes, Road Runner stays one step ahead of his foe, causing the Coyote to walk into all his own traps. And for some reason, the vindictive, ruthless Coyote has our heartfelt sympathies as we watched him walk into his own death traps over and over, never getting wise to the Road Runner's clever defense systems.

We must become like Road Runner. We must be ever vigilant and alert, always outsmarting self-sabotage, which left unchecked, will rob us of happiness and peace, ultimately threatening to undermine a beautiful God Story in the making.

Altar Your Plans

One of my favorite sayings is, "every *no* is really a *yes* to something better." More than twenty years after writing the first edition of this book, I can say without fail that God has always rewarded my trust in His goodness. Whenever He has asked me to give up something, He has always given me back something better! God doesn't ask us to give up in order to deprive us, but to prepare us to receive more fully and completely.

"Now wait a minute," I hear you object. "What if I never get the chance to experience an incredible love story in this lifetime? Jesus clearly said that we wouldn't be married in the next life."

That's true in a sense of how we understand marriage now, but our idea of earthly marriage is very limited and simplistic. I do agree that we will not have the same kind of limiting, imperfect marriages that we have here on earth, but I fully believe, based on my studies of Jewish perspectives on Scripture (and reason), that we will have the opportunity for even greater intimacy and relationships in the future Kingdom or realm (perhaps even offspring, which seem to be at the heart of Creation)—something that will make marriage here seem really basic! This is in God's character, and He has given many promises to the effect! God is the God of intimacy and relationships ("it is not good that the human should be alone...")! Putting deepest desires on an altar now is merely offering it to God so that He might give it back in highest and best form in His perfect timing and form!

My younger self didn't know much about any of this when initially writing this book. At that time in my life. I still had a lot of sorting out to do in my heart about the character of God, which can only be learned through time of life and experiences. Like Abraham, I was at that sort of altar where you aren't sure of the outcome but you're trying to believe that God will make good on His promises.

Without a doubt, I knew it was time to offer up the very things I had longed for, in order for God to bring them back to life, just as He did for Abraham. Best decision of my life!

Ditch the Hollywood Daydream

Late fall of 1998, just prior to my ex-husband's wedding; God began to reinforce some important boundaries concerning future male interaction. At this point, I was finally ready to listen. After the past fiascos, I realized that it's better to be physically alone and happy, than in a wrong relationship, emotionally and spiritually drained and feeling alone.

Primarily, I believe He directed me not to consider an emotional relationship with anyone unless He made it clear to me that He was leading me into marriage with that person. Otherwise it would be pointless, meaningless, and a waste of time and energy, as I had experienced the times before. Plus, any relationship God wasn't leading me into would be a threat to my "white rose" promise—which I believed to be a specific man God was preparing for my future.

In order to pass the tests, there were a few more deceptions I was going to have to be able to recognize and reject in the moment. The first was flattery. Julie's definition of flattery: *A way for a man with bad intentions to make you think you're special, in hopes of getting something from you.* All my life I was a sucker for it.

Another lie to be overcome was Hollywood's gross misrepresentation of dating. In Hollywood, dating always starts out extremely fun, light, romantic, with heart-warming music

The Table of Hope

playing in the background. He's always a hunk; she's always a hot, skinny, fashion statement, and they look amazing (perfect?) any time of the day or night. They are never sick, clumsy, awkward, needy, or less than charming, but usually do have one little conflict of some sort to keep things interesting. They usually have sex on the first date, don't worry about birth control or STDs, have no difficulties with sexual performance, and she is never on her monthly cycle. The conflict is always resolved just in time for the end of the movie, at which point they get married and live happily ever after in a storybook house most of us only dream about.

Obviously, my lifetime experiences (and the experiences of everyone I know), haven't matched the above scenario even remotely. On the contrary, I've noticed that most relationships ended up characterized more by trial than triumph, sucking up precious time and energy in ways that aren't healthy or life-giving. There is hardly ever such a thing as a fun, energizing, amazing dating relationship outside of a patient approach characterized by genuine love and respect for each other's wellbeing throughout. Feelings get involved, sex often becomes the focus, people get hurt (including dads), and it takes a lot more emotional energy than planned.

Before getting deflated and dismayed, remember: True, pure, beautiful romance is alive and well! We will look at an example soon, but first, there was something I had to do.

Pass the Test

In November I went to Florida to visit a friend in the same area where I lived after college during my first marriage, and where both of my girls were born. On my returning flight out of Tampa, Mr. TDH (tall, dark, and handsome) Businessman started flirting with me at the check-in counter. Suddenly I was alerted to the sound of alarm sirens and red flashing lights. Was airport security arresting a vicious criminal? No. It was my flattery receptors under full alert. They had spotted a man with bad intentions.

The Perfect Fit

The old me would have interjected, "Wow! This man has noticed me. By all the attention he's giving me, I deduce that I am valuable and special." But the "new vigilant me" (NVM) saw right through the whole thing and I almost chuckled at this gross underestimation of NVM's recently acquired radar skills. Very detached, I watched as he hotly pursued me, trying to bait me with verbal and non-verbal messages that I was special, that I was beautiful, and that he had a lot to offer me—*for a night.* How disgusting! What a lie! This time, I didn't even entertain it. I'd have to give the guy an "A" for persistence though. Although I wasn't encouraging his attention, he wasn't about to give up that easily. He actually changed his seat assignment so he could sit by me on the airplane, so I decided I would make use of our "special" time together.

As flight attendants and other passengers craned their nosy ears in our direction and made frequent passes by, I nicely grilled him (hold the BBQ sauce) for a while with objective questions and observations about how he was hurting his wife, his children, and most of all God—who he claimed to have a relationship with. I told him my story, and how my life used to be bound up in lies, like his still seemed to be.

Watching him loosen his tie for the umpteenth time (grills can get pretty hot) while I sipped limey V8, I told him how I had been set free from that empty life, and I would never return to it for any price. He had absolutely nothing to offer me in light of my newfound joyful security and identity in God.

After backing the Devil into a corner—somewhat speechless and sweating, I might add—I politely excused myself and found another seat, several rows toward the front of the plane. Once off the plane in Denver, I ran all the way to my next gate without looking back—okay, partly because our arrival was late and they held the next plane home for me. But more importantly, I symbolically fled my old behaviors, and my old nature, without a backwards glance. I knew God had given me a way of escape, because I was looking for one. In the past, I wouldn't have run, I would have stayed to hear what my itching

The Table of Hope

ears wanted to hear. I would have tried to figure out how close I could get to red-hot briquettes before I got burned.

A real change had taken place in me. Stone by stone the old dam of lies crumbled, letting the refreshing waters of hope and restoration come flooding in. I felt like I had proved to God that I was ready to do it His way. I committed in my heart that the next man I allowed myself to get into an emotional relationship with, if there ever was one, would be *the man* God indicated to be my husband.

I know you're waiting to get to the part about the earthly romance. After all, that is why you probably bought this book. I will not disappoint. Let's get to the juicy details!

The Perfect Fit

Step 2: Assembling the Border

Now that we've got our foundation of faith in God's goodness in place, it's time to get on with the picture—the inspiring romance. After turning over and organizing all the pieces, God's next step was to begin putting the border into place. The border is always a good starting place and reference point. Even though I couldn't tell what the picture was going to be, I was so happy *something* was happening—even if it was just the first stages!

The Perfect Fit

From Here to Timbuktu
(God's Best Will Find You)

My first introduction to Steve Ferwerda was in March of 1998 via a Christian singles site, around the same time I met Matt and Tom, when I wasn't supposed to be dating yet. In addition from the feeling that trying to make my own contact with someone was "getting ahead of God," I didn't think He would use man-made technology to bring about my romantic destiny. Wasn't that trying to reduce God to a formula? Something just sounded wrong about punching the qualities you want in a mate into a computer and immediately seeing all these date possibilities pop up—like a big dating buffet. However, the Christian singles possibilities in the Rocky Mountain region turned out to be more like a starvation diet than a buffet, with very few selections to choose from.

At that time, Steve was checking out the "low-cal" selections himself, and thought it was pretty funny when only one girl showed up on his screen from the state of Wyoming. When he wrote me a letter, he made it clear that he wasn't looking for Internet love, just making new friends. That was quite a switch from the other two men. I wondered what was wrong with him. The two letters we sent back and forth in March were less than compelling, and our ways parted seemingly for good.

Beauty Salon Surprise

Four months after our introductory letters in March, Steve was traveling through my hometown in Wyoming, and remembered one detail from our brief correspondence—that I worked in the hair salon at the local Holiday Inn. On a sudden whim, he veered into the hotel parking lot on his way through town, curious to see what kind of a gal would be making her home in this isolated Wyoming town. Was she worth getting a look at? There was only one way to find out.

Walking into the hair salon, he looked about as comfortable and confident as a woman in an auto parts store. To make matters worse, we were in the middle of a shop meeting. All talk

The Perfect Fit

ceased and five sets of curious eye stared him down from the little group in the middle of the room.

"Can we help you?"

"I came to see Julie." He looked around nervously.

"Did you want a haircut?" One of the girls asked him with a tone of understanding. *One of my haircuts was enough to make anyone nervous!*

"Ah...no, I wanted to speak to her outside for a minute."

All the other shop employees smirked and snorted, casting assuming glances at me. Although not surprised, I was embarrassed by my co-workers juvenile conduct. It was Friday and they had their usual case of end-of-week giddy behavior.

"I'm Julie." My flushed cheeks belied my calm manner.

Wondering what in the world this was about, I led him out to escape the nosy stares and obnoxious snickers.

We stepped into the dimly lit hallway, and I looked up at him with curiosity. I certainly had never seen him before. He was tall, brown hair, blue eyes, with an athletic build, and—well...*kinda cute!* Maybe he was here to tell me that I had won that fitness contest I entered. *No, too serious.* Or maybe he was the estate attorney for a long lost rich aunt. *No, too casual.* Or perhaps he hit my car in the parking lot. *No, not serious enough.* Several thoughts went through my brain, trying to figure out the purpose of this mysterious stranger.

Clearing his throat, he introduced himself, "I'm Steve Ferwerda. Do you remember that we wrote a couple letters back and forth a few months ago? I was just cruising through town and remembered you work here, so I thought I'd say hello."

"I remember vaguely." I smiled at him, thinking I must have made a lasting impression in those letters for him to go to all this trouble to meet me. Staring down at a pink gum wrapper someone had carelessly thrown onto the floor, I felt *completely flustered and at a loss for words*—a rare moment for me, indeed!

"I thought maybe we could grab a bite for lunch."

"That's a nice offer but I really can't. We just started a shop meeting and I have to be there." *Besides, I'm not going to go to*

Assembling the Border

lunch with a man I wrote to four months ago whom I've had not interaction with since. Kinda creepy.

"Well, maybe some other time then..." he hesitated, as if hoping I would give him more options.

"Yeah, maybe so. Well, thanks for stopping by, Steve. Have a safe trip."

After we parted, my co-workers nosily inquired, "Who was that hot guy and what in the world did he want with *you*?"

"Very funny! Just for that, I'm not telling."

My brief exchange with Steve was short and awkward, to say the least. There was no "love at first sight" or spark of anything between us—well, unless you count the "fireworks" that came next.

Fireworks in August

About a month later Steve wrote to me again in August with an uncommon request. He suggested that he come down and go to church with me some Sunday, and perhaps afterward go on a hike up in a nearby mountain canyon together. Since I was getting pretty wise on the lines used by men and on their *real* motives by this time, it sounded like the perfect pick up line for another man with bad intentions. At least he hadn't started using flattery yet. Who knew? His intentions could lead anywhere from a sexual advancement to a downright dangerous crime plot.

I emailed back to him, jokingly serious, that chances were slim to none that I would go on an isolated hike with him—even if he let me bring my gun. For all I knew he could be a dangerous criminal hiding behind the guise of an innocent church boy. It was a little suspicious that a single guy in his thirties would ask a gal he barely met once, if he could drive three hours to take her to church. I didn't know any men that would drive five minutes to go to church with me. Likely story. He'd probably "run out of gas" on the way, "just miss church" and show up just in time for the big "love hike." Fat chance! Besides, how did he know so much about the hiking possibilities in our local mountains? He wasn't from around

The Perfect Fit

here. Maybe these Internet relationships were more dangerous than I thought!

Already a bit distrustful of him, the real sparks ignited in his letter that followed. He admitted he had a real hang up with my "divorced with two kids" situation. We weren't even talking about dating and he already let his general prejudices toward divorced people work abruptly into his letter. He let me know how a woman "like me" would conflict with his dating ideals.

Even though he tried to not sound like his preconceived notions about divorced people were directed at me specifically, he made some pretty judgmental assumptions that invoked a fiery response. The nerve of him to say those things to me—I could certainly see why he was still single! And even if some of his assumptions and judgments had a ring of truth, he didn't have a right to so carelessly fling them at me without any love or compassion to balance the fact that life and relationships can be messy, and unplanned things happen in life, even if you don't want them to.

The mission was assigned. It was my job to set him straight...with pleasure. Writing him back with an equal lack of love or compassion (it's always so much easier to see someone else's fault in a matter), I blasted him with a short novel, pointing out his judgmental assumptions and attitudes toward me, and divorced people in general.

So, that was the end of that! I knew I would never hear from him again, but at least I had gotten in my two cents. I thought maybe I did him a favor in the long run, perhaps helping him to have a better chance with any future encounters he may have with divorced women. Hopefully he would learn how to address his concerns with more diplomacy and gentleness. After all, the chance of him meeting a woman who had never married at his age was pretty slim! After pushing the "send" button on my email, I rubbed my hands together, leaned back in my chair, and gave a satisfied little cackle.

Assembling the Border

Humble Pie Ala Mode

You could have knocked me over with a parakeet feather when Steve wrote back an equally lengthy letter of humble apology for his unfair and thoughtless remarks. It was downright shocking! He admitted that the letter was a "little judgmental." He said he didn't mean for things to come across like they did, and he wished he had re-read the letter before he sent it. Do you know how rare it is to come across a man who will admit when he is wrong? I thought there might be hope for him yet. *Well, maybe he did have a proper upbringing after all,* I piously thought to myself while hastily pushing the delete button to erase his long painstaking letter.

Mission Impossible

It would have literally taken a miracle for me to ever find my future "perfect fit" on my own, under the circumstances. There were a few single men around town all right: Burley Bruno, the mega-tattooed biker down at the local bar; and Cowboy Clyde who would probably sing "Achy Breaky Heart" to me for eternity, and worse yet, Grandpa Elmer who relied on Geritol® and a cane to get through his day. How was God going to accomplish this miraculous meeting with an available godly man who was also a good fit for me? The prospects seemed pretty grim. My pastor assured me that if God had to bring someone into town from the next state over or even from across the world, His plans would be accomplished. My only job was to be steadfast *today*...doing what I am supposed to be doing where I am supposed to be doing it.

I happened to notice in the lives of men like David, Joseph, and Daniel, that the more hopeless things looked in their circumstances, the closer and more spectacular the resolution. What good would a divine miracle be if circumstances were already humanly solvable or not that dire? The only prerequisite for being in position for a miracle is that a miracle is the only solution. Without Heavenly help, there is no silver lining, no hope, or no way out. Throughout Biblical history, the day things looked the very worst—downright awful and completely dark and hopeless by human standards—was also the day the whole story changed by Divine intervention, but not a minute before.

I had seen that reality over and over. When God wants to display His power and glory to humans, He arranges the backdrop of impossibility into our lives and circumstances so that He is our only hope. If God could part the Red Sea when the chariots were a stone's throw from the Israelites, and make a lonely shepherd boy a king, and bring Joseph out of prison to be second in command over all of Egypt to save a country, and keep the mouths of hungry lions closed for Daniel, and feed five thousand on just five loaves and two fish, if He could make Peter walk on water, Abraham become a father at age one hundred, and Lazarus rise from the dead, why couldn't He fashion a miracle-inducing plan into my life as well? Surely He could arrange the coming together of two lives—two lives that would bring an inspiring reflection of His love to the world.

My reference point of hope was still that white rose. Its magical appearance and fragile beauty reminded me every day from my kitchen that God had a beautiful, awesome, fragrant plan waiting for me that I didn't want to ruin. I believed my hope wouldn't be disappointed. The expectancy and anticipation that drifted into my life was fascinating. Strange occurrences were taking place and I was paying attention.

Pleiades Perspective

One crisp October night, I had been invited to attend a meeting at a local crisis pregnancy center, where I happened to meet a beautiful auburn-haired woman. Jackie and I hit it off right away, and she invited me to stay around after the meeting to get acquainted. During the course of our conversation, we got onto the subject of her marriage. With little prompting, she recounted this beautiful unfolding romance about how she and her husband met and were led into marriage by God's leading.

For some reason, Jackie didn't spare the cherished and miraculous details she saw God arrange to bring her marriage together—the mutual respect and purity in their dating relationship, the inspiring purpose they experienced together as

Assembling the Border

a result of their union, and even how God moved them beyond seeming insurmountable obstacles before their wedding. She didn't elaborate on this part of her story, but focused on the inspiring outcome.

I marveled at how Jackie's face lit up as she shared the details. Her story was even more fascinating than the cross-dresser convention I accidentally crashed once at a hotel in Cincinnati. The best part was how this story dropped into my life so unexpectedly! Straddling wooden bar stools in an outdated blue-wallpapered kitchen with a perfect stranger, I wondered about the significance of this "chance" meeting. It stirred something in my soul that longed for that kind of story in my life.

Until now, I didn't even know these stories existed in real life! I was captivated by the genuine, selfless love that characterized their relationship. I wanted to give a big cheerleader Herkie Jump. Jackie proved to me that true romance is alive and well—even more real and satisfying than the Hollywood counterfeits! I felt as if I had made a great discovery of something that I'd only suspected and *hoped* was possible. God had revived romance—His version of romance—in my heart.

I remember the first time I looked through a powerful telescope. Without its aid, I saw a very limited number of stars and constellations. But then I looked into that telescope and...wow! The heavens were indescribably vast and magnificent compared to my previous awareness with unaided vision. I gained a whole new perspective as I beheld galaxies, planets, moons, rings on Saturn, and different types of stars (Betelguise is amazing!). That experience was enough to teach me that there is always more beyond what we can see or imagine. In this situation with Jackie, God put that telescope up to my eye, giving me a new perspective through her story. It was not only possible that there was more to godly romance than I'd ever seen; it was a reality!

Through Jackie's story, I learned that joyful, attainable romance exists, and it's far better than any misguided and deceptive fairytale (except maybe Shrek's), but only through patience and commitment to saving oneself for the better thing.

I wanted that kind of story—the kind where you know without a doubt that God did it. It made me even more determined to hold out for God's plan of good for my life. I just hoped he wasn't a big green ogre with enough ear wax to make his own nightly dinner candle.

Learn How to Tell Time
(The Right Thing is the Right Time)

One Saturday afternoon in late October, I was working at the salon when a daughter of one of my clients came in for a haircut. This young woman lived in Denver and she came home for a weekend visit. During our conversation, she made a bizarre offer. A friend of hers worked at the local airport with service to Denver, and she indicated that her friend could get me buddy passes on the local airline if I ever needed to go to the city for any reason.

We gals are always getting ourselves in hot water by saying too much, too impulsively. I was sure this was one of those times. First of all, they weren't *her* hard-earned flight passes, I didn't know her friend, I barely knew her, and all I did was give the girl a haircut. Sure...yeah, like, I was going to call a complete stranger, who probably had dozens of friends and relatives coming out of the woodwork to get in on free tickets, and say, "You don't know me but...one of your friends offered me your buddy passes. *You don't mind do you?*"

Secondly, what good would buddy passes do me in this situation? I wouldn't go to Denver without my car, that wouldn't make sense. I'd have to pay just about the price of an airline ticket to rent a car to get around while I was there. Wondering if the airport girl would appreciate how generous her buddy was being with her buddy passes, I decided not to take her "flighty" offer seriously.

Assembling the Border

Opportunity Knocks

Winter is for the penguins! Personally, I think global warming is a marvelous idea, and that we should all use more hairspray. But in the interest of becoming a more well-rounded person that year, I decided to try an attitude adjustment. After all, God did create winter, so there must be *some* redeeming quality about it. I just had to find out what it was. I called up a girl friend and she and I decided to take up skiing together.

I heard a rumor that skiing was expensive, so I wasn't sure how dedicated I was to trying something I knew I'd hate anyhow, especially on my limited budget. After all, why would I want to actually pay a bunch of money to spend all day out in the freezing cold blizzard conditions, exposing my limbs to possible frostbite and amputation, collecting icicles in my nostrils (this actually happens in Wyoming), donning twenty five layers of clothing, and all the while trying to learn how to like something about winter. I was just about to give up on the idea when suddenly, I recalled a distant memory that someone had invited me up to ski free at a small ski area where he worked winters in the mountains of Wyoming. Steve Ferwerda!

Being the opportunist that I am, I thought to myself, if I can get a hold of him and I'm nice to him, maybe he'll give us some lift tickets! Then I can freeze my limbs off for free! Besides, maybe after the judgmental letter incident, he will feel guilty and want to make it up to me.

I was pretty sure I had deleted any records of him, but I looked anyhow and found that I still had him in my recycle bin. Starting with some friendly chitchat, my letter skillfully and subtly worked up to my schmoozing agenda. As I pushed send, I wondered if he would respond affirmatively, not at all, or just get it over with and mail me a package of chocolate covered anthrax bars. Oh well, nothing risked, nothing gained.

He wrote back about a week later and told me he was no longer in Wyoming, but had relocated to Denver in search of a different job. He apologized for not being able to provide the tickets, and asked how things were going. I answered him in a

The Perfect Fit

like friendly manner, which surprisingly started a series of short but light-hearted letters back and forth.

Since we are both quite competitive, we tried to one-up each other with our humor and puns in every entertaining letter. In fact, I made a thought-provoking and frightening discovery about his sense of humor. It was identical to mine! I didn't have to explain any of my puns or jokes to him. This was indeed a real anomaly because my humor doesn't jive with 85% of the American population. Of course, his clever wit was no match for mine, but his letters were more entertaining than watching a man shop for curtains.

As the letters continued, we also began sharing what kinds of things God was doing in our lives. I was still a little skeptical because I had heard too many men who could "talk the talk" *about* God but really didn't have an intimate connection *with* Him.

A Like Heart

Early November, I mentioned the dating principles God had placed in my heart in recent months. Steve agreed with my newfound convictions, mentioning a book he'd read called, *I Kissed Dating Goodbye*, by Joshua Harris. He also told me about how he was currently getting to know a girl in Colorado and that he wanted to keep things platonic between us. Argh! The nerve of him to even suggest that I had other intentions! By this time, I wasn't even thinking "relationship" with anyone, and certainly not a guy who was this impressed with himself.

Even though I was offended by his implications, I had to admit that a good-looking Christian guy like him, encountering a bountiful supply of desperate single women, would need to be cautious and upfront so as not to lead anyone on. Admittedly, I was a little bit intrigued to meet a man in this day and age committed to a similar patient approach to dating and emotional involvement, even if it was this exasperating Steve Ferwerda character.

There was a real sincerity about Steve's letters that gave me the feeling he wasn't just putting on an act, that he really did

Assembling the Border

have solid values. *If there is one guy out there with these kinds of convictions and values, I wonder if there could be another one out there somewhere for me? Maybe God put him into my path to encourage me that these men exist—even at my age (32).*

I figured God was also offering me a chance to have a completely platonic friendship with a desirable man, something I had never done before. It was remarkable to not be pressured for something more, or to get my hopes up for more. I was gaining insight from Steve Ferwerda and I did look forward to his humorous letters that made my sides hurt from bouts of hysteria, much to the curious gazes of my children playing nearby.

A Working Vacation

Remember my test with Mr. Tall, Dark, and Handsome in the airport on my return trip from Florida? The trip to Southwest Florida took place the middle of November when Steve and I were writing each other frequently. I knew God had arranged the trip, because it turned into a key event in healing from my divorce. I had spent eight of the thirteen years of my first marriage in southwest Florida, and felt as if I needed some closure from this significant portion of my past.

The trip plans started when a good friend of mine from Florida called and invited me down to see her. She said she missed me and wanted me to come down, so she was paying for my airline ticket! There was no way I was going to turn down a relaxing, sunny beach trip in the middle of winter. The day my friend called me to invite me down; I called my travel agent to begin checking airfare.

"There must be something weird going on," the travel agent told me when her computer generated the fares.

"Why? What's wrong?" I asked with a worried tone.

"Well, the fares are the lowest I've ever seen them. Either someone made a big mistake or Someone else is watching out for you. Let's book it before it changes!"

The Perfect Fit

Mistake? There are no mistakes when God is working His magic. He owns the airports on a thousand hills—oh and the cattle, too.

If I thought I went to Florida for a nice little relaxing beach vacation, God had other plans. Since such a large portion of my marriage had been lived there, I had difficult memories and issues that needed to be faced in that setting. With a heavy heart, I took on the hard work of facing my past failures and lost dreams, learning new lessons from old experiences, and seeing things from the past with a changed perspective.

As hard as it was, I saw God working out things for good all around me that week. I was even invited to share what God was doing in my life with a Sunday school class at my old church. That in itself was daunting because I fit into that high statistic "would rather get hit by a speeding bus than do public speaking." The class had about fifty people in attendance, which looked more like—gulp—at least a 150 from up front. But when I got up to speak, I was filled with an amazing peace, and inspired with a message about trusting God's work and goodness in our lives, despite mistakes and difficult circumstances. I felt equipped to clearly speak from my heart with the message and the ability to do what He asked me to do.

After the class, a couple women come up to ask me for some reference material that I shared and to tell me how much I encouraged them. It was so wonderful to feel God's power in my weakness, enabling me to share my story-in-progress with others. Not very relaxing or comfortable, but very exciting. After the trip, I had a great sense of accomplishment. It seemed like a whole year of healing had happened in one week. God used it to set me free from my past, and to prepare me for something special in my future, which for all I knew could be just around the corner.

A Narrow Miss

Before I left for my trip, Steve and I had discussed (through our letters) the possibility of getting together for a friendly lunch in Denver at the airport on either end of my trip, even though I

Assembling the Border

only had about a forty-five minute lay-over each way. I knew from past experiences that a friendly lunch was next to impossible. But then again Steve had proven his intentions toward me over the past month of correspondence. Not once had he hinted at anything beyond friendship with me. However, our conversations were getting longer and more compelling all the time and I knew he was feeling just as curious as I was to set eyes upon each other again.

Even though my will was having its usual tantrum to do my own thing and give in to temptation, my heart didn't feel right about getting together with him yet. Meeting Steve at the airport and trying not to get charmed by his good looks might be like me trying to resist chocolate chip cookies hot out of the oven—not very good odds. Why set myself up for failure? I didn't want to rationalize under the guise of friendship because I didn't trust myself. I told God that I believed He could arrange another opportunity for us to get together later, if it was *His will*, and I would say no to *my will*. So I told Steve I didn't think it would work out at this time, but I didn't tell him why.

I was ever conscious of the fact that it was only another couple of weeks until my ex-husband remarried, and it was not worth getting ahead of God. He simply wanted my trust and patience. I felt exhilaration like never before over the new life I was living in more empowered choices than defeat. Newfound truths budding in my heart were really helping me to resist unhelpful temptations for the first time, something that wouldn't have been possible even a few months earlier.

When I returned home feeling quite encouraged and restful, observing that God was busy at work in my life, there was a parcel of mail waiting for me. I opened it to find Steve had sent me the book, "I Kissed Dating Goodbye." This is the same book he'd told me about that encouraged *courtship* (basically hanging out as friends and waiting single-heartedly for God's leading to progress into romance). I was surprised and delighted that he went to the effort to send me such a gift! I read it in about three days, and it totally confirmed and restated some of the convictions God had already put in my heart through prayer and listening to Him in the months before. I encouraged myself with the thought once again: *If Steve has these values, there MUST be another guy like him out there somewhere.*

And so, the tender green shoots of hope continued to grow. Within the pages of that book, I had even more opportunity to study authentic love. In my circles of friends, I didn't have many living examples of those who had invited God to participate in their dating lives and marriages. Starting with Jackie and now from this book, I was starting to see a pattern of what a God-inspired relationship looked like. Even in the book, Joshua Harris had opportunities to be with Christian girls that he could have rationalized were adequate as a choice for a mate. But he was waiting for a special adventure, something he knew God initiated. He was waiting to see God's hand moving him into, and then throughout a relationship.

After getting settled that night, I discovered there was also email waiting for me from Steve, telling me that he tried to surprise me at the airport, but that I forgot to tell him which day I was flying back. When discussing my schedule before, he knew the airline and time, but I had inadvertently left out the particular day. He told me he even contacted the airline, but came up with nothing. Hmmm. He sounded pretty curious to me. Thankfully, he was unsuccessful in his attempts—it was a narrow escape!

These men seemed relentless in tempting me to compromise my vows, but I was still very determined not to let it happen, no matter how great Steve seemed. In all fairness, Steve didn't know about my decisions not to date until my ex-husbands impending remarriage. Since we weren't contemplating a relationship, the topic hadn't come up.

After the separation from my husband, I had a circle of advisors that helped me through the ordeal with counseling, accountability, a listening ear, and many a proffered shoulder for my tears. Among them included my sister and brother-in-law—strong influences, volleyball partners, and deep friendship ties in my life. Also were Pastor Charlie and his wife, Bonnie, a professional counselor who worked with me and the kids, and

Assembling the Border

also a mentor from college. They all helped me keep my head on straight spiritually and emotionally.

None of these people (especially my sister and her husband), had approved of my recent relationships, even though they were Christian men; they all told me I was out of God's will and timing. But for a time, my strong-willed streak took over and I didn't listen to them. God used my trip to Florida to finish humbling me and to give me a contrite heart toward the people that had tried to help me, despite my rebellious attitudes.

After the trip, I went straight to my sister's house and broke down in tears, admitting to them my willful stubbornness, in spite of their repeated attempts to help me make the right choices. They were put in my life by God to help me be objective and stay on the right path, and I had refused their wise counsel.

Proverbs says that a man (or woman) who refuses wise counsel will come to ruin (Proverbs 10:8). If I hadn't turned away from my insistence of trying to run my own life, that's exactly what would have happened. The caring representatives of God's love in my life that they were, they weren't trying to take away my fun. They saw the counterfeits trying to steal my future and they were trying to love me with protective truths. I hadn't wanted to listen to them, but now I stood in their kitchen, asking their forgiveness. I cried, they cried, and our relationship was restored over yet another box of Puffs®.

Step 3: Filling in the Middle

Have you ever had the sense that something big was about to happen in your life? With the foundation laid, the border set in place, now the real visual progress could begin! However, filling in a puzzle can be painstaking and lengthy. Sometimes when those middle pieces are being filled in, you get so caught up in certain colors or patterns, that you aren't able to see the big picture. Certain pieces seemed almost impossible to find. Sometimes you even wonder if pieces are missing.

With God, no pieces are lost, but the going can still be slow. Every now and then while He was working on my puzzle, I had to take a step back to give my eyes a rest from straining so hard to see the details. From this angle, things began to make sense...progress was being made. Come take a look!

The Perfect Fit

Don't Cross the Line
(Stay Friends for Now)

November 27th, 1998 was a death...and a day of new beginnings. It seems the two usually go hand in hand in this life. This was the day my ex-husband closed the door of reconciliation when he remarried. It was time to go forward by making peace with my past, so I invited a friend over to be with me for a special rite. We sat on my couch by the crackling fire while I wrote out on a piece of paper all my old dreams that had never seen the light of day. I then symbolically wadded up my dreams, and threw them into the fire where they curled up into a shrunken black mass, and finally dissipated into ashes somewhere on the bottom of the fireplace. This rite of passage was my permission to start over and let go of the past.

An Open Door

Sitting in Pastor Charlie's familiar office the next week, we contemplated my ex-husband's remarriage, and his words took me by surprise.

"Julie, I want you to know that I am very proud of all your efforts. You have listened to my suggestions, and followed my advice toward the goal of reconciliation to the best of your ability—even when you didn't feel like it. I know you've had some setbacks, but it's a growing process for all of us. The important thing is that you have finished strong and grown immensely as a person. From this point on I want you to know that when the enemy comes to call, trying to pester you with shame or guilt over your failed marriage, you can use this truth against him: As far as I am concerned, the burden of guilt is off your shoulders and you can live your life with a clear conscience. You have made every effort at reconciliation with your ex-husband, and my wife and I are your witnesses."

The Perfect Fit

> "No weapon forged against you will prevail, and you will refute every tongue that accuses you. This is the heritage of the servants of the Lord, and this is their vindication from me," declares the Lord. Isaiah 54:17

What freedom his words brought! I was never more grateful for all the hard work and submission to his advice than in that moment. Even though I had pursued those two relatively short relationships lasting about six weeks each, ultimately those didn't factor into the outcome of my ex-husband getting remarried because he had been involved with another woman since before our breakup. If his heart had been even remotely interested in reconciliation, he would have ended that relationship to try to salvage our marriage. With my Pastor's assurance, I could indeed move forward with a clear conscience.

A Timely Interruption

I was perfectly fine the day of my ex's wedding. As is common in the healing process, however, where I was feeling happy and content thinking about my hopeful future one day, the roller coaster of human emotions brought me back down to the bottom the next day. Twenty-four hours later, I was a completely depressed mess, convinced that my life was eternally unfair and all the fun was over.

After all Lord, I was the one who tried to make things work, and here he is married and seemingly happy while I'm alone.

It was evening and I was sprawled on my bed, gushing like a faucet, dumping out all my losses and complaints to God. Despite my pitiful state of mind, I reminded myself to hang on to hope, even when it seems impossible. I preached a mini-sermon to myself that God had a plan for my life, and not to let my feelings start dictating my actions again. More baby steps in learning to trust God, defeat those old negative thoughts patterns—especially self-pity—and let God solve my problems. I'm sure it sounds a lot easier to do on paper than it actually was at the time!

Filling in the Middle

Hugging yet another box of Kleenex, my prayer was interrupted by the telephone. I didn't recognize the number. *Probably a pesky telemarketer—great timing as usual!*

Not caring squat about how nasally and pathetic I sounded, I picked up the phone.

"Hullo?" I sniffled, stuffy from crying so much.

"Hi, Julie. This is Steve—Steve Ferwerda." He sounded a little hesitant. "Did I get you up or something?"

"No, I was just...ah...just sitting here giving my Kleenex box a work out."

"Is something wrong? I can call back later if it's not a good time."

"No, I'm fine. Thanks for asking. What are you doing?"

"I thought it might be nice to finally talk to you on the phone. Arthritis is setting in from all that typing and I thought maybe we could give our fingers a rest for tonight. Besides, I have trouble keeping up with your long letters. Are you a professional writer or something?"

Laughing out loud I thought, *If only he knew!* He continued, "You know, I really just wanted to talk to you. Our letters have been so much fun and interesting. I've never been able to have such great conversations with the girls I've known before. You are so easy to talk to and almost as funny as me!"

At his complimentary admission, the inflating giddy feelings in my chest could have made a blowfish jealous. This didn't seem like flattery; it was different than the kinds of lines I was used to—more sincere somehow.

After quite a while of lighthearted chitchat—and a lot of laughing—we got onto the topic of our families. I could hear the longing in his voice as he talked about his parents, who lived in the Middle East. Steve and his two brothers and sister had all spent their growing up years mostly in Beirut, Lebanon—all the way across the world—before coming to the States to go to college. His parents had settled in Lebanon as missionaries, and were still living in that area.

The Perfect Fit

Hmmm. Pastor Charlie's words echoed in my mind. So he's from the next state over AND from all the way across the world. Very interesting.

"Do you get to talk to your parents much?"

"Not very often. My mom sends me letters but it's too expensive to call much, and I only get to see them once a year at the most. You know, I really miss seeing them. I know they pray for me, but we are so far apart. It's not like I can just go home..." he stopped short, his voice wavering and distant. "I'm sorry, I just get lonelier for them around the holidays," he said, his tears more apparent now.

"Of course you do. I can't even imagine what that must be like. It sounds like your Mom and Dad are really great people, and I know they must miss you a lot too. Are you close to your siblings?"

"Yeah, but I don't get to see them very often either. My brothers are quite a bit older and busy with their families. Plus, we're all pretty spread out. I have an older sister closer in age who was my main playmate when we were kids. She used to force me to play with Barbie's and crochet doilies with her. It was torture!"

"Oh, you poor thing...having to play with that sexy, blond, bikini-clad babe, driving her pink corvette around the living room."

"Well, I did play with G.I. Joe too," Steve tried to reconstruct his masculinity.

"It sounds like your sister had a profound impact on your formative years. It's comforting to know you can crochet a doily for me if I ever need one."

Our phone call lasted for at least an hour and a half, but the time went by so quickly that it seemed more like ten minutes. The open and easily flowing conversation was such a contrast to the rocky start we had in the beginning of our friendship.

The timing of his phone call, interrupting my lonely prayer, stuck out like a snow cone machine at a hot summer fair. Even though we'd been writing letters steadily for almost two months, I really didn't know very much about this guy. But what I could

Filling in the Middle

tell so far is that he appeared more real and genuine than the guys of my past, because he wasn't trying to impress me or to get anywhere with me. He wasn't even interested in me *that way*—he was already in a potential relationship with a girl in Denver. Besides, I wasn't ready for anything yet. And I was sure that, although God has a sense of humor, He wouldn't be so mischievous as to have me get together with another Steve—the same name as my ex-husband.

Email Invitation

A couple days later, I informed Steve by email that I had to go to the southeastern Wyoming town of Cheyenne the next weekend to deliver some cats I'd been taking care of for a friend while she moved. I was really tempted to ask him if he wanted to get together, mostly because I was growing ever more curious, but I knew in my heart that I was prone to getting ahead of myself again.

When it comes to rationalizing my own desires and going my own ways, I have the word "prone" stamped on my forehead! But this time, I wanted to be *completely* patient for God to move, believing that He could arrange whatever He wanted for me. In fact, I rested in the belief that He wouldn't let me miss His best for me if I was daily trusting and waiting for His direction.

Settling the matter in my heart, I didn't mention any possibilities in my letter. Steve emailed me literally a few minutes later and he suggested that he come up to Cheyenne and go to dinner with me Friday night, December 4th. I felt very peaceful about that suggestion, since my ex-husband was now remarried, and since Steve was a nice guy with the same values. And since Steve had initiated the meeting, I thought it would be appropriate to have a friendly dinner with him. His current relationship was a good safeguard for our feelings.

I really wanted to continue learning how to be friends with a guy without expecting or hoping for anything more to develop. He was so easy to talk to, and I found myself looking forward to the invitation. I was curious to see him again, because I couldn't remember what he looked like. When you're writing letters almost daily to someone it's nice to have a picture in your mind of whom you are talking to. All I could remember was the impression that the view would not be disappointing!

A Dinner to Remember

On the way to Cheyenne the next Friday, I was attacked with a case of the stomach bug. Had I not already driven half way there before the bug set in, I would have turned around for home. I even had to get a hotel room for a few hours in a town called Rawlins. Just going through Rawlins is enough to make a person feel under the weather, where average wind speeds might be 60 mph. It's a cold, dusty, sage-brush infested prairie town in the middle of nowhere that boasts of the highest suicide rate in Wyoming—probably because constant typhoon-like conditions set people on edge. It's also home to most of the state's criminals, but in my opinion, they don't need a prison. Just *living* in Rawlins would be punishment enough without steel bars!

Even though I had to hang out in Rawlins for a while, our dinner wasn't scheduled until the following evening, so I had plenty of time to get there. The next night, however, we almost didn't get together AGAIN because this time, Steve wasn't feeling very well. At the last minute he decided to drive up anyway—a two-hour drive—just for dinner with me.

When Steve came up to the door of my friend Vicky's house, I was giving a last minute haircut to her husband, so I couldn't answer the door. Following Vicky into the kitchen, Steve's tall frame and broad shoulders filled the doorway, a boyish grin shyly spread across his face.

When I said I couldn't remember what Steve looked like from the summer before, I must have blocked it out so I could function properly the rest of the workday. Suddenly, hands shaking violently, my mind was on anything but the haircut at hand. My victim was lucky to have his ears still attached when I put my scissors down. *I know, I know.* I shouldn't have been focusing on these things, but who wouldn't? I couldn't take my eyes off Steve's beautiful, beaming smile, twinkling blue eyes,

Filling in the Middle

and his, gulp, broad, muscular shoulders. We all have our weaknesses, you know?

"Are you ready?" he asked.

"Yeah, sure. Let me get my coat."

"Hey, what about my haircut?" my abandoned project yelled across the house.

"Haircut? Oh, yeah. Your wife can probably handle it from here. She did a great job on the dog with the clippers this afternoon," I said, handing her the clippers.

"No way! I'll hold out till you get back!"

Following Steve out the door, I silently chided myself. I already knew Steve was funny and interesting. Why did he have to be so dang handsome, too? Since we were only going to be friends, I was hoping that he could be sort of homely. But alas! His wholesome, athletic, boy-next-door look was a total chick-magnet in my book. *Whoa rein it in, girl! This is just a friendly dinner. You are going to have to ignore appearances. This might be another test. You've come too far to blow it now.*

Shivering from the cold, we took our places across from each other in Chili's at a dimly lit table. After removing our coats, we got so intent in conversation, we forgot about ordering. The waiter was getting a little huffy after the fourth time by our table, so we finally took a break to order. Chitchat was flowing as easily as the water in our glasses, and we were having such a great time together that the hours and, it seemed, the wait shifts flew by. A dinner tip doesn't go far when you're splitting it with three different waiters, but it was a cold winter's night and we didn't have anywhere else to talk.

There was something different about this guy sitting across the table from me...his sincere expressions and warm manner. It just seemed so...comfortable. We were like two old friends picking up where we left off. Maybe it's because there was music playing in the background just like at the movies. Maybe it was all a trick, or a test. Only time would tell.

This guy (with the same name as my brother *and* my ex-husband), who grew up across the world and now lived in the next state over, didn't have any noticeable differences in beliefs

The Perfect Fit

on spiritual matters. We had the same sense of humor, we liked the same foods, we both liked to travel, and we liked many of the same sports. The more we talked about, the longer the list of similarities grew. It's a little weird to say, but I felt like I was talking to myself.

Mid-dinner, a guy I knew from a college campus ministry fifteen years earlier happened by our table and I recognized him.

"Hey, Don! What are you doing here?"

"I'm living here now." He looked at the floor, trying to figure out what to say next. Don and I had known each other fairly well back in college and had even gone on a mission trip together. In college Don was super shy, especially around girls, and blushed just about anytime a girl even spoke to him. He hadn't seen me since our college days, when I was married to my previous husband, and he was unaware of anything about my life before or since my divorce.

"Uh, Don, this is my friend...Steve." Awkward! With a puzzled expression Don held out his hand for the introduction. Probably thought I was out having a fling. The silence that followed hung as heavy as cigarette smoke in a bowling alley. I didn't exactly feel like I could explain the situation, so I didn't even try. Instead I changed the subject.

"So what have you been up to these days—what sort of work are you doing?"

"I'm a doctor."

"No kidding! It's not really a big surprise though, you always were smart! What kind of doctor are you?"

"Well, I'm a...uh...ghnhcohhgist," he said, so mumbled I couldn't understand him.

"What was that?"

"I'm a...gynecologist." He blushed profusely.

Don...*a gynecologist*? What do you say to your shy college buddy, who blushes about a girl rolling up her sleeves, when he tells you that he is now a gynecologist? The irony of the moment was mind-boggling. In typical Julie fashion, not sure what else

Filling in the Middle

to do, I asked the first thing that popped into my mind. "Oh, wow. Do you like it?"

Did I just say that? As soon as the words left my lips, I could have dived under the table, never to be coaxed out again. Instead I just nervously shredded a napkin or two in my lap, pretending that it was a perfectly normal question. The poor guy.

"I guess so," was all he was going to admit to. After what seemed like a mortifying eternity, he politely left.

Steve had already picked up on the situation and snickered right along with me after Don left the restaurant. In fact, we laughed so much that night we were probably a nuisance to nearby tables. Everything seemed so funny! Being with him that night was such a breath of fresh air after feeling so uncomfortable and unnatural with Matt and Tom. Steve echoed my sentiments, admitting he could talk to me more comfortably than anyone he'd met before. I guess you could say being together that night felt like putting on a comfortable pair of old slippers. *Okay, God! What's going on here?*

An Impulsive Offer

Right before the holidays, Steve and I were discussing plans on the phone. I was sort of anxious to see him again and wondered what he was going to be doing. "Are you spending Christmas with your brother's family this year?"

"Yeah, probably. We usually spend it together. So what are you doing?"

"We're going to spend the holidays at my parent's house as usual. It's a blast! With our crew and my sister's family of six, there's always plenty going on. The cousins have a great time together and we all stay up late and play games, eating ourselves into oblivion. My Mom's an incredible cook. Anyhow, it's always cozy and fun."

"Wow! That really sounds fun." Was that longing I heard in his voice? Probably not. He had his own family to spend the holiday season with. But what if he was hinting? Before thinking, I blurted out, "Would you like to come up and spend it with us?" The question hung between us for an awkward moment.

Scatter Your Skeletons
(Reclaim Grace)

As soon as the words left my mouth I could have kicked myself. I didn't want to sound that forward and besides, he had his own family living near him in Denver. Surely he would rather spend it with them. I'd just set myself up for rejection.

"Yeah, that would be great!" He chimed in, before I could lament too long. He sounded genuinely enthusiastic about the invitation, but I wondered why he would accept when he already had plans. Immediately, however, I uncovered his real agenda.

"Julie, one more thing before we hang up," Steve nonchalantly broached the subject. "Does your mom by any chance keep Breyer's® mint chocolate chip ice cream around?"

Was this a trick question? Was there a wrong answer? Little did I know that he was scheming for some new, unsuspecting suppliers. I had no idea that he liked to worm his way in to hearts and homes near and far to freeload on ice cream, which I later discovered he liked to eat after every meal. He had probably worn out his welcome at all the homes of single gals in Colorado.

"She might." I made a mental note to call my mom and make sure she was prepared for her soon-to-be houseguest.

The Opal Redemption

This time I was upfront with my wise mentors. I told my sister and her husband right away about the fact that Steve was coming for Christmas. God must have been working in their hearts, because my brother-in-law, who protected me like a watchdog, was unusually receptive.

Including the two catastrophic relationships mentioned earlier and my marital unfaithfulness, I felt like I needed to share with Steve the mistakes and scars of my past if there were

Filling in the Middle

any indications our relationship was going to progress further. It was important to me that our friendship be built upon honesty from the start, in case something more were to develop between us at a later date. If that day ever came, I didn't want my past to be an unknown stumbling block to him. Besides, God was calling me to a new life of openness and transparency, and He was trying to teach me not to be afraid of condemnation over my past. God was bigger than my past, and bigger than those who tried to keep me in it. I'd come to understand that no one could legitimately hold my mistakes over my head since God had forgiven me and I'd turned away from those behaviors.

Even so, admitting these things to someone like Steve—a seemingly lily-white missionary kid—was going to be a bit agonizing. I was afraid of his rejection but I knew it was only fair to tell him the truth. The question was, how was I going to approach this most difficult subject in a way that he would understand my heart and realize how much I had changed? The remorse over my mistakes was great. But in another way I didn't have regrets because my mistakes had grown me into a better version of myself.

> And we, who with unveiled faces all reflect the Lord's glory, are being transformed into his likeness with ever-increasing glory... II Corinthians 3:18

While sitting in church the Sunday before the big event, I asked God to show me a way to talk to Steve about my past, if that is what He was ready for me to do. I guess God was ready because not two seconds later, an unusual solution flowed through my thoughts directly and specifically.

God took me back to a time in high school when my Dad brought me a beautiful opal necklace from Australia. Gifts from my Dad were beyond rare (this might have been the first one), so this was a very treasured and sentimental piece of jewelry in my collection. I'd never learned how opals are formed, but I was about to. Right then and there, disrupting my attention to the morning sermon, God gave me the notion that the answer to my dilemma was found symbolically in His dynamic opal creation.

The Perfect Fit

He impressed upon my thoughts that the magnificent, radiant beauty of an opal is formed as a result of flaws and devastation...just like my life.

Not sure exactly what He meant by that, I did some research later online. In an oversimplified explanation, opals are formed near large cracks (faults), or blows (areas of heavily fractured rock) in the ground. The cracks and blows provide a path for water to deposit silica, and then under heat and pressure the resulting beautiful stone is formed. Do you see? The cracks, flaws, and areas of devastation provided an opportune *location*. Heat and pressure provided the right *conditions* for the formation of the magnificent opal.

It wasn't hard to relate this to my life. I had the opportune location of cracks and flaws—imperfections, failures, unexpected blows of life, fractures of mistakes, and ultimately brokenness. Some of them I caused; some of them I didn't. People had certainly hurt me and let me down, many circumstances didn't turn out the way I wanted, and in addition, I had just plain made a mess of things.

I also had the right conditions of heat and pressure, God's refining fire in my life—convicting me of my wayward tendencies, filling me with useful grief over mistakes that hurt myself and others, allowing disappointments and ill-treatment by others to shape my character, purging old unproductive habit patterns—using it all to mold me into Julie 2.0.

The result? Radiant, colorful, fiery beauty refracted from His light shining upon those devastated areas where He had restored me. It was not my doing; I just provided the right condition of brokenness to make a path for His cleansing waters to flow into my life, depositing more radiant character qualities. His heat and pressure were applied carefully and in just the right amounts, turning those ugly places into redemptive beauty. It was all to display His miraculous work and His redeeming power in my life.

To sum it all up in one sentence, my failures, weakness and darkness plus God's grace, love, and light are able to bring about brilliance and beauty unparalleled. *It is all about God and*

Filling in the Middle

His intent of good for all His children. My important job was to be a *willing* receptacle and then to shine out my newly given brilliant colors under the ray of His light.

And that was the opal lesson interrupting my attention that fine Sunday morning. My earthly father gave me the opal; My Heavenly Father gave me the potential for an opal life.

The directness and clarity of His Words brought a measure of comfort and reassurance about the dreaded task at hand. So the next question I needed answered was, when? I was completely dependent upon God's timing, not trusting myself to initiate this delicate conversation. I told Him, "If You want me to talk to Steve *this* weekend, You have to clearly show a sign between You and me. I will wear my opal necklace all weekend, and if Steve says exactly, 'That's a pretty necklace,' I will know it is You giving me the go-ahead. Otherwise, I won't say a word until You appoint the time." From the quick response in church, I had a feeling that now was going to be the time.

True to my instincts, the first full day of Steve's stay at my parent's house, we were sitting in the living room after breakfast when Steve studied me for a moment and said, "That's a pretty necklace." I even wore a collared shirt that day, trying my best to conceal it as much as possible.

Digging my fingernails into the couch, I muttered under my breath in exasperation. *Okay, You win God! But did you have to do it so, so...first thing?*

Was it my imagination or did I hear in response, "My grace is sufficient for you, for my power is made perfect in weakness" (II Corinthians 12:9)?

At the Well

I managed to drag things out until later that evening, just in time for Steve to share some starkly contrasting things about his past before I could get in my confessions. We were sitting on a bed in the cozy second story guest room, reading some recent letters from his mom, when we got into a discussion about our lives.

"Steve, there's something I want to tell you about—"

The Perfect Fit

"Me, too! Before I forget...did I tell you about the 'Purity Test' that I took at work the other day?" I listened in frank disbelief as he continued on, telling me about a test that was shared by his co-workers to determine a person's level of purity—a number one being a saint, and higher scores all the way to a hundred reserved for those who have really experienced it all. It might have been funny any other time.

"So what did you get?"

"Oh, it doesn't really matter."

"Aw, come on! I won't tell anyone."

"All right. I'll reveal what I scored if you promise not to laugh. I scored a four."

Somehow I managed to laugh with him on the outside, but on the inside, a battle was waging. *This is not good, not good at all!*

"I didn't tell anyone at work. Can you imagine how they would have reacted? I would've never heard the end of it from Joe who works next to me. 'Yo, Steve, you're not doing enough *scoring*, if you know what I mean. You gotta get out there, live a little. What do you do for fun, man?'" Steve's imitation of his co-worker's attitude was both funny and sad at the same time.

"What did your co-workers score?"

"The next closest score to mine was a thirty five! They teased that person for several days because most of their scores were up in the sixties or seventies, with a few even into the nineties."

Thinking of how my own score would rate, I braced myself for what was ahead. "It is sad that they gloated over high scores, but you do realize that you scored even lower than most Christians would?"

"Yeah. I realize I'm different than most, but I don't take credit because I know God has really protected me through the years. Anyhow, most people's standards these days are so different than what Christ wants for us. It calls for a radical commitment against the flow every moment of our lives. In hindsight, I wish I had revealed my test results to the others in my department, but I guess I was just afraid of the ridicule that would have followed.

Filling in the Middle

Something struck me as significant about what Steve had just revealed about himself. A virgin at age thirty-two, he was lily white by anyone's standards in today's world. Memories of a certain white rose landing in my clasped hands surfaced. Could the white rose be more cryptic—more a symbol than a literal form?

"Now, what was it you were you going to tell me a few minutes ago?" Steve's words cut into my thoughts.

Oh yeah, he had to remind me. If I wasn't nervous before he shared the big news, I sure was sweating now. Not only was I contending with his judgmental words about divorce from our early correspondence, but now this! An impossible four out of one hundred! That was just what I needed to hear before I stepped back out on the ice of trust. I had visions of Steve's shock, disgust, and unbridled gasps. Could a four handle my relatively high numbered confessions?

Memories of past rejections loomed over my head like a mousetrap, ready to spring. But if I wanted to be truly free of my past, I had to get it over with. Taking a deep breath, I began to openly and honestly recount my story using the illustration of the opal. As I inserted the details of my past; a strange and supernatural phenomenon began to fill the room.

"I have swept away your offenses like a cloud, your sins like the morning mist. Return to me, for I have redeemed you." Isaiah 44:22

I imagined myself back in time at a place I had never been before. It was an old watering well near a dry, dusty town; passersby had dwindled off for the day as dusk fell, except for the one man who stayed behind for a drink. He knew my name and everything about me, it seemed, as we sat there talking much more honestly than you would expect from perfect strangers. There was something about those eyes—something accepting, inviting. I knew somehow I could trust Him. As I began opening up about my pain and struggles, he began asking questions in the right places. He listened to me pour out the confession of my mistakes, for which I had no defense.

The Perfect Fit

And then he did something amazing. Eyes brimming with unconditional love and grace, he gently looked into my face. "Woman, where are your accusers? Are they here to condemn you?"

"No sir." I answered, staring at the ground.

"They don't condemn you, and neither do I." His kind and gentle words touched me deeply with healing. Falling to the ground in relief and gratitude, my tears flowed freely, washing His feet.

> [Jesus said] "Do you see this woman? I entered your house; you gave Me no water for My feet, but she has wet My feet with her tears and wiped them with her hair. You gave Me no kiss; but she, since the time I came in, has not ceased to kiss My feet. You did not anoint My head with oil, but she anointed My feet with perfume. For this reason I say to you, her sins, which are many, have been forgiven, for she loved much; but he who is forgiven little, loves little." Then He said to her, "Your sins have been forgiven. ...Your faith has saved you; go in peace." Luke 7:44-50 (selected)

Taking my hand tenderly in his, Steve looked intently into my eyes. "Julie, I just want you to know that, no matter what mistakes you have made in your past, you are a beautiful person to me because of how God has used those things in your life to shape you into who you are today. I love your heart, Julie. I love what God has done in you. I want you to know that I see you with a 'tabula rasa.' Your slate is clean—you are pure as a virgin in my eyes. That is how God sees you. That is how I see you."

The words were familiar. Almost exactly the year before, sitting in church one Sunday, God spoke words to me out of Jeremiah 31:3-4: "I have loved you with an everlasting love; I have drawn you with loving-kindness. I will build you up again and you will be rebuilt, O *virgin* "Julie." Again you will take up your tambourines and go out to dance with the joyful." God spoke my name in place of Israel because He had wiped my slate clean, and to Him I was as pure and clean as a virgin.

Filling in the Middle

I didn't think any human (besides my mother) could have treated me with so much grace and respect that night, especially someone like Steve Ferwerda, unless the very grace of Jesus came through his heart to mine. Through Steve, God gave me a real and tangible assurance of the way He felt about me.

Now that I had come clean, I could relax. My past couldn't be used against me anymore. My skeletons were out of the closet and scattered on the carpet of grace. They couldn't threaten me or hold me in bondage—I was free!

After the amazing talk, I came down the stairs *crying*! My Mom took one look at me when I got to the bottom of the stairs, and panic swept across her face. She had seen this look before. "No, not again!" she cried out in exasperation, misunderstanding my tears. I broke into laughter and explained to her that these were "happy tears," not the "skunk blues!" With a mischievous grin on his face Steve came along behind me, "Let's have some more ice cream!"

Just Like the Movies

That Christmas we had a fresh blanket of powdery snow. The view out of the large picture windows throughout the house displayed velvety-white mountains, which only contributed to the cozy effect of being stranded indoors next to the roaring fire, kids chattering and playing together, mounds of delicious food, and an occasional football game blasting from the TV.

The atmosphere was warm and happy, but it is difficult to put into the words the additional peaceful and comfortable feelings Steve and I had around each other that weekend. Our ear-to-ear grins would have made the Kool-Aid pitcher guy jealous. I was trying hard not to presume anything, but being in his presence felt a lot like that feeling you get when you come home after a long and wearisome journey. Still, we were both careful not to forge ahead emotionally. In fact, while it was obvious that we were both enjoying the budding friendship, things were actually progressing quite slowly compared to past relationships. The pace was...well...rather *romantic*!

The Perfect Fit

We took walks, had a snowball fight, drank plenty of hot chocolate, played cards with the fam, ate enough ice cream to dimple a thousand thighs, watched movies, and stayed up late talking together every night. It felt like we *were* in a movie except that there was no music playing, unless you count the kazoos the kids blared in our ears...oh yes, and the song in my heart.

The ice cream in Steve's bowl wasn't the only thing melting that weekend. My Mom's heart warmed up to him nicely, too. It was worth giving Mom's intuition a try since my Dad blew it with Pe Pe.

A Real Sob Story

When all the grocery stores were out of Breyer's, it was time for Steve to head back to Denver. A couple of hours away, he called me from Rawlins (the same town I mentioned earlier), hardly able to speak for uncontrollable tears. I tried to comfort him and told him I'd be crying too if I had to go to Rawlins.

"It's not thththat," he said between great gasping sobs. "From the minute I left your house, I haven't been able to stop crying."

"Was the food and company that bad?"

Steve laughed in between gasps. "I don't know how to express it but I've had this unusually happy feeling in my heart after being with you."

"Yeah, you sound so happy!"

"God has really been speaking to me about this weekend and I'm just overcome by these intense feelings."

"What has He been saying to you?"

"I can't say exactly, but this isn't like me. I don't usually cry and now you've heard me cry twice in a month! Anyhow, thanks for being so sweet to me this weekend. You are one of the most amazing women I have ever met. I miss you already."

"Aw. I was just putting on a good show," I tried to lighten the conversation. "But I do miss you, too, even though we've only been apart for two hours now." I wanted to add, "I think you need a nap."

Filling in the Middle

"I better get back on the road. I will call and let you know when I get to Denver. Thanks again."

I know how a person can be unaware of the effects that driving to Rawlins can bring upon them, so I could really sympathize. As soon as he got to Denver he would return to his senses. Still, it was very sweet to have him call to share his sentimental feelings with me.

Divine Travel Arrangements

Just before leaving, Steve invited me down to go skiing with him over New Year's weekend, five days later. It looked like I was going to get some free ski after all. With only a few days to prepare for the trip, I began to contemplate the six-hour drive to Denver through treacherous winter conditions. *I wish there was another way, like flying or something. Flying! That's it! The buddy passes I was offered to Denver might still be an option! It wouldn't hurt to ask!*

I got a hold of my client's daughter by phone and told her my situation. She told me she had already mentioned it to her friend who worked at the airport and it was a thumbs up! All I had to do was to make the phone call and let her know when I wanted to fly.

"No way!" I couldn't believe my good fortune.

"Way!"

I hung up the phone in disbelief. Did God orchestrate this? *Whoa Nelly. Not so fast. This could be a polite offer that falls through.* How many times have I got my hopes up for something and it didn't pan out? Still, it was funny how the thought dropped into my head just as I was searching for a better way. *God, I know that I don't have things figured out. If you want me to use an airline ticket please work it out. If you don't want me to go at all, please show me.*

I hesitantly dialed the phone number scrawled on a piece of paper, waiting for a perfect stranger to answer so I could throw out my extravagant request. It was a little awkward to say the least. When she answered on the third ring, I stuttered through my request.

The Perfect Fit

"I'm a friend of Vanessa's. She told me to call you and see if I might be able to use one of your buddy passes to Denver sometime..."

"Oh, yeah, I've been expecting your call. It's no trouble. When would you like to use one?"

"I was hoping to fly down on Wednesday afternoon so I could get out before New Year's Eve," I requested meekly.

"Yeah, that's just fine. A little warning though. This is the busiest weekend of the year so you may have trouble getting a flight out."

"No problem. I really appreciate your letting me try. That is so generous."

"You can use as many as you like, so just let me know when you need them. I'll go ahead and put your name on standby this Wednesday afternoon. See you then."

Could somebody say, "amen—galory halleluiah"? You don't get these kinds of things for free. That is, unless you are being scammed...or unless God is moving people and circumstances to conspire in your favor for a divine purpose.

Three days later I stood on the small concourse of our one-airline terminal, seating assignment in hand. The check-in agent had already cleared my stand-by ticket for seat availability on one of the busiest flight days of the year. It was a little daunting to have to sit in cargo, but what did I expect for nothing? On our little regional prop planes, there isn't actually much distinction between cargo and coach class anyhow.

When Steve came out from hiding behind a payphone near my gate to surprise me, my heart nearly leapt out of my chest with joy at the sight of him. His warm bear hug assured me that he was glad to see me too. Ever since our memorable time together at Christmas, I secretly began to hope that God had other plans for us than friendship.

After countless letters and hours on the phone over the last two and a half months, with no pressure for a romantic relationship, I felt a special kind of trust and familiarity growing toward this man. I could barely contain my excitement about the four days together that lay ahead of us. Yes, this would be an incredible weekend. Nothing could possibly dampen my spirits.

Don't Be Late For Your Own Funeral
(Keep Your Security Above)

After spending a couple days down in Denver while Steve finished up his workweek, we were ready for the New Year festivities to begin. Our weekend destination was a super-cozy mountain home nestled among deep snowdrifts and pine trees near Breckenridge, Colorado. It was owned by the middle-aged couple Steve temporarily lived with in Denver. Terry and Sandi had practically adopted him as their son, letting him enjoy all the family privileges, including the use of their mountain chalet. They were planning on following us up for the weekend, but couldn't get away from the city until later in the day.

The Ugly Truth

Making the two-hour drive up the mountain this fine New Year's Eve, it seemed to be the start of a perfect, light-hearted weekend with the perfect, romantic backdrop.

Ah, this New Year is finally full of promise and mystery. My storybook ending is finally on its way. Smiling happily in the light of the moonbeams illuminating the car, I relaxed back into the passenger seat. I marveled at how easily this relationship seemed to be falling into place.

Cutting into my blissful thoughts, Steve broached a harmless sounding topic of "expectations." He had my full attention as I thought over our relationship thus far, sure that he was going to let me know just how perfectly I was fitting into all his dreams and expectations. After all, the time we spent together these past two days had been fun, relaxed, and without even a hint of conflict. Steve had seemed a little distracted, but he worked through New Year's Eve Day while I found other things to do. Nevertheless, he'd been sweet, attentive, and seemed to enjoy himself as much as I did the past couple days.

The Perfect Fit

But now, shrouded in the safety of darkness, he obviously had something difficult he needed to say to me.

"Julie, I'm struggling with something. I was wondering if we could talk about it."

As he spoke, I clenched my purse, hearing a hint of rejection. "I'm listening. What do you have on your mind?"

"I have to be honest and admit that I'm having some doubts about where this friendship is going. I mean, you aren't exactly the type of girl that I imagined marrying someday..."

"And what type of girl is that?"

"I guess I still am just sort of hung up on your past—being divorced with kids and all. I've waited all these years...saving myself...for someone without so much...baggage."

"I thought you said you loved what God has done in my life *because* of my past...and that I have a 'tabula rasa.'"

"Well I did say that, but I just have these other times that I feel differently. I guess I'm saying that I imagined myself with someone a little different."

"It's not like we're getting married! We're just friends." I reminded us both, cracking a playful smile his way.

There it was again. Baggage. The word of the day that kept resurfacing. Just a few days ago he told me between sobs how much he liked me—baggage and all. Now he apparently felt like I was touting enough baggage for an airport carousel. Relaxing the death grip on my purse, I was relieved his confession wasn't as bad as the heaviness his voice conveyed. Understandably, it was sort of a loss of dreams for him. My baggage was a loss of dreams for me too.

Steve had only had one truly romantic relationship in his whole thirty-two years. He'd waited long and hard for his future mate. After all that time, he had built up certain ideals and expectations of what he thought God's best for him would look like. It was really no different than the way I'd been imagining how I would get a white rose. Where I had only had a year to ponder my ideal visions—he had spent at least ten years thinking about what he wanted.

Filling in the Middle

Many times our expectations or ideals are based on warped perceptions from the impossible illusions created by others (e.g pop culture) or our envisioned fantasies. It can take a process to set our mind on what is real, true, and lasting. Steve was in that process of learning a higher, better perspective on what is important and desirable. When God's best fit for Steve came on scene, he would have to trade in his cherished dreams, expectations, and desires, trusting that God would give the best thing for him.

What surprises You have in store for us when we let go of our own agendas and plans. How better could You surprise Steve than by giving him something he doesn't realize he wants?

I was confident that, in time, my baggage wouldn't be such a deterrent to him. In fact, a good weekend together was just what he needed. He would soon see beyond his tainted expectations and realize that my love for God and charming personality were enough to overcome any negative perceptions he might have. Besides, I could already tell by how much he was staring at me that he was mesmerized. Our mutual attraction would give the relationship the momentum it needed until he really saw my heart. Problem solved. Relaxing back into the seat once again, I slipped into warm comfortable thoughts.

Steve broke the long silence with some encouraging words, focusing on the positives he saw in me. "Julie, I think you're a wonderful person. Your love for God is so genuine, I really appreciate that."

See, what was all the fuss about? He's coming around already, I thought to myself, leaving the door open for him to finish his thought.

"Like I've told you, I can talk to you easier than anyone I've ever met—and I love your sense of humor, especially your crazy puns. We've had some great times together. I don't think I've ever been as comfortable around a girl as I am around you."

My thoughts swung like a pendulum, thinking how easily he had overcome his own objections. But then, in the light of the moonbeams, I noticed tears streaming down his cheeks. *For Pete's sake! What now?*

The Perfect Fit

Wiping his sleeve across his face, I could tell he wasn't done yet. Either there was going to be a "but" or he was having a sentimental moment about meeting the girl of his dreams.

"...But I have to be honest about something. I don't know how to say it but, I...I...I'm nn--nnot att--ttracted to yy—yyou." He finally stammered the words out like a jackhammer, breathing a sigh of relief at having gotten this burden off his chest.

There was a "but" all right. I should have recognized he was buttering me up to go in for the kill—like giving me some powdered sugar with my arsenic, Kool-Aid with my cyanide. When he admitted *the ugly truth*, it plunged through my insides like a knife.

I handled it really well, though. I didn't force him out of the speeding vehicle or throw him down a steep embankment. I might have attempted it if he wasn't the one driving. I felt completely humiliated, insulted, and angry. My injured self-esteem and protective pride inwardly shrieked, "A*nd who do you think you are, God's gift to women?*"

My heart turned as cold as the winter scene outside. I couldn't seem to stop the anxious trembling and sick feelings taking over my body. Trying to make sense out of what he said, I nursed my pride. *Argh! Steve Ferwerda is clueless! He must either be blind or stupid!* I couldn't ever remember any man being so openly rejecting or brazenly hurtful with me. When I didn't respond, he tried to explain his feelings further, expanding his newly dug hole into a spacious grave.

"I'm sorry, Julie. I know you must really feel hurt about this. I do, too. I know this sounds really shallow, but part of my struggle is that I never pictured myself with a brunette."

A brunette? That really narrows the options. Is he saying he would rather be with a blond? In my mind, I finished his thought for him. Well, Julie, I was sort of holding out all these years for a girl like Barbie—that long blond hair, ocean blue eyes, shapely figure. Frankly, compared to someone like you, she is actually quite desirable. Besides, she has all the latest toys!

Filling in the Middle

Playing with her all those years in his sister's room, he must have imagined himself next to her in the pink corvette, or lounging around the pink mansion, or camping in the pink Winnebago. That perfect, idealistic fantasy girl made him promises she couldn't keep and left him with a fixation on blonds, I was just sure of it. With the intensity of my feelings raging inside, I couldn't trust myself to speak. The horrible silence that hung between us for the rest of the trip seemed as loud as a freight train.

Barbie Wins Again

I never did like the obviously male-designed Barbie. She doesn't play fair. Barbie is probably the culprit for starting the "Blond Revolution"—the multi-billion dollar business in the hair care industry. There's absolutely nothing realistic about Barbie, yet in light of this obvious factor, I felt inferior.

Brown—my hair is brown. Yes, I know brunette Barbie's came about after the social uprising over discrimination, but we all know who is more prevalent in designs and more superior in sales now, don't we? I don't have all the latest recreational toys or a pink convertible, and my figure isn't 45-18-38. *Wait! I have got to stop this lunacy. I am comparing myself to a six-inch plastic doll!*

It's pretty pathetic and dehumanizing when you start competing with a doll. It was irrational, but I felt so hurt and disappointed at this new turn of events. Baggage can be overcome, but lack of attraction? And his timing obviously wasn't thought out. He could have at least waited until the end of the weekend to deal this crushing blow! Then I could crawl home with a crumb of dignity intact. But as it was, I was trapped. I had nowhere to go for two more excruciating, long days. I had to stay and squirm, pretending to be okay.

After Steve's moment of honesty, doubt set in. Was I supposed to be here? Did I get ahead of God again and misunderstand His leading because of following my own will? God's will for me certainly wouldn't have these kinds of trials, would it? With my eyes, things didn't look good. And right then

The Perfect Fit

I decided, no matter what, I wasn't going to impose any expectations or pressure on Steve, or let him know how deeply he hurt me. If he saw the hurt, he might guess at the underlying emotions that had taken root in my heart.

Hiding my feelings that night was like trying to levy up the banks of a storm-swollen river. In light of the lie I believed that the positive attention I received from men over my appearance had something to do with my value and worth, the proverbial carpet had just been removed from under my feet. All along I had hoped this New Year's beginning was going to be different, but already it was turning into one more disillusioning relationship to add to the pile.

Picture Perfect Model

Steve further widened the gap between us the next evening when he unknowingly answered my previously unverbalized question. Yes, he really did think he was "God's gift to women." While we were sitting by the fire, he pulled out old photo albums he'd brought along so that I could see glimpses of his past. Next he brought out *the catalogs*.

"Did you know I'm an "international ski model'?" He enunciated the words in a macho voice, wagging his head from side to side in his best celebrity playboy imitation. Through furrowed eyebrows, I gave him a blank stare.

"Take a look at these," he said pulling out some old outdated ski catalogs, proudly showing me each picture from his modeling days. I might not have given it a second thought before this weekend, but under the circumstances, I found some clarity on the weekend. Looking at the catalogs—all five of them—carefully enshrined in their protective plastic covers, I realized he thought I wasn't good enough for him. No wonder he saw me with such a critical eye! He wistfully looked over each picture, proudly giving me the details of each one.

The whole thing was so ludicrous; it would have made a great sitcom episode. After politely listening to his detailed explanations of each pose from his brief modeling career, I stood

Filling in the Middle

up, yawned, and made it clear I was ready to escape to my room.

Truthful Reminder

What are you trying to do to me God? I asked while getting ready for bed that night. Instantly, a memory flashed through my mind. One night a few months earlier, when I lay my requests for a future husband before the feet of Christ, I asked Him to include my number one desired character trait—honesty. The years of living with many forms of dishonesty from my ex-husband left a wake of devastation and scars. Add to that, the flattery and more dishonesty I'd encountered from most men before and after my marriage. I was used to being told what I wanted to hear from men most of my life. This was a very destructive pattern that did not help me to live in the real world. I needed to learn how to hear and accept the honesty of others. Since I was trying to live an honest life myself, I told God I wanted to find someone else who also tried to live the same.

But Lord, I didn't realize this is what honesty would look and feel like. Does it have to hurt this much? The lies and distortions were easier to swallow for the moment. Just because I asked for an honest man doesn't mean You have to give me one! And anyhow, since when did you start giving me what I ask for? Have you thought about that trip to Tahiti?

When I'd given that request to God, I'd only thought of honesty as a beneficial trait and had forgotten how the honesty of others could also be painful. If I had to admit it, Steve's honesty was both frightening and refreshing to me. I had never met a man who was so willing to be truthful, even if it caused pain. His honesty didn't just hurt me; I could tell that it really hurt him to have to admit those things to me, too. God pointed out to me that I had to keep the bigger picture in mind, and that in the long run, honesty is always better than flattery. I couldn't argue that.

God, do you think you could tame it down a bit, though?

The Perfect Fit

A Martian's Defense

Before going on, I want to defend the alien (sometimes referred to as Martian) in question. I know you're thinking, "How shallow! What a jerk! How could she even be interested in a guy like that?" Well, I was having those same thoughts exactly.

Since Steve had not participated in the dating game during his bachelor years, he hadn't practiced being smooth, or telling a girl what she wanted to hear to get what he wanted from her, like some other men were good at doing. When Steve admitted his feelings to me in the car, his voice betrayed the anguish he felt over the whole thing. I knew he didn't really have anyone else to talk to about these conflicting feelings, and they were weighing him down emotionally. I believed he sincerely enjoyed my company, but his eyes were dissatisfied. In spite of my hurt and anger, I also felt compassion for his confusion and disappointment.

Perhaps Steve did have a lofty view of himself, but who doesn't if we're being completely honest? I would certainly be a hypocrite if I didn't admit that I have unjustified, elevated, shallow thoughts about myself frequently. I unconsciously demonstrate superior attitudes every day. Maybe I don't carry around my previous beauty queen pageant pictures (I know, so vain), but I certainly give preference to myself often and think I deserve better than what I'm getting much of the time without giving a thought to the best interest of others. It's absolutely no different, but maybe I'm just a little better at covering it up.

Heck, if I'd ever had an opportunity to model for magazines, I probably would have wanted to show them off, too. He did look good in those actions shots, skiing down rugged terrain. Like I said, Steve just wore his heart on his sleeve more than most people, but it doesn't make his offenses any worse than anyone else's. I was just the "lucky" girl who got practice learning how to deal with it.

Despite his verbal blunders, I believed that deep down, Steve was genuinely a quality guy. He was worth giving a chance, as long as the door appeared to still be open. God could use our

Filling in the Middle

weaknesses to help each other become better people. Perhaps Steve could gain some skills in being less critically minded and a little more sensitive, and I could gain some new skills in standing firm in my God-given, unshakeable worth. I knew Steve had a really teachable heart so I was sure he would be willing to let God work on these areas of his life. But would a teachable heart be enough for this situation if God did want us together? Steve had choices to make too, and he could miss a divinely orchestrated provision if he wasn't willing to follow God's leading. This was definitely a God-sized challenge.

Death at Dawn

Under normal circumstances, I would say that no man is worth losing sleep over. However, I lay awake all night that first night, replaying events and wrestling with my deeply sad feelings of rejection. Even though I didn't know God's plan for the friendship, I found myself not wanting to give up the possibility of Steve being a part of my future. I thought Steve was such an incredible guy in so many important ways. He was the first secure, quality man I'd met since my divorce that I could actually imagine spending my life with, even though God had given me no indication I should think about Steve this way. He was exactly my type, even if I wasn't his type!

Consuming thoughts that I wasn't good enough, or pretty enough resounded in my head like a beating drum. Depressing voices tried to get me down in my greatest place of vulnerability by attacking my value and worth. There had to be something more than the way you look to draw a man's heart initially...something more lasting. What was the secret of winning a quality man and keeping him? I didn't know the answer, but I hoped someday soon I would find out.

Reliving my "white funeral" once again, I lay around in my coffin for a while before closing the lid. I wasn't quite ready to be buried yet. My will struggled hard. Did I trust God with my future enough to let Steve go? I thought I wanted a man like Steve Ferwerda, but is this what God wanted for me? Did I believe that God's best for me was better than anything I could choose for myself? Was I going to let all my previous months of hard work and sacrifice go to waste, trying to take back my own will again? Despite the desperate and painful screams of my will, it was time once again to show no mercy.

God, no matter what—if Steve doesn't want me, or even if any other man doesn't want me, You are my number one and I know You want me. You are my only hope and security. You are all I really need, and I am going to trust You. If I lose everything else in the process, You are still worth it all.

Finally at dawn, I closed the lid of the coffin and buried my will once again. With the first rays of morning light streaming into my bedroom, I was able to finally let go of the feelings of rejection, humility, and dread of facing the next day. It was enough to make any Road Runner proud!

Find Beauty in Honesty
(Inner Strength is Alluring)

Green looks good on broccoli, but I don't think it's really my color. After Steve admitted his lack of attraction for me, an emotion I had never experienced before emerged—envy. Starting that weekend, every time I saw a beautiful woman—or any woman with certain features I thought might be desirable to Steve—I coveted them. I hovered, watching Steve like a hawk out of the corner of my eye, checking to see what women he noticed. Then I compared myself to these women, feeling completely inferior if they had any feature I deemed better than mine. I was so pathetic that actually resorted to pointing out little flaws on other women, trying to cast shadows on them while trying to make myself feel better.

"That girl sure has big legs, I wonder if she ever considered lumberjack leg wrestling. ...Look at how the light reflects off her thinning scalp, where are my sunglasses?...You could put a whole pencil collection behind her ears. ...Breath mints were invented for her. ...You could rest your laptop on those two big surgical implants she's flaunting!"

Filling in the Middle

This was so not like me! I was ashamed of how low I stooped to put others down in order to try to feel better about myself, but the mean competitive thoughts overwhelmed me. I couldn't bring myself to appreciate the beauty in other women like usual. It was one of the worst conscious prisons I have ever been in, and I could hardly stand to be in my own skin.

By the comments I hear around me, I realize now that many women live in this same prison. Many of them have had trouble getting the approval they crave from the prominent men in their lives. Others know that their husbands are looking around at other women, comparing them unfairly, and they live in a joy-stealing furnace of jealousy and insecurity. We live in a society that values appearances over everything, despite the fact that outward beauty is fading for all of us and is no indication of our worth. It's a very difficult battle that many women face daily within themselves.

Consider human nature. Let's pick on Hollywood. You can find almost any successful male movie star with the most incredibly beautiful wife at home, and read about how he cheated on her or left her for another woman. If appearances really can satisfy, why does this happen? Why would a guy look somewhere else when he has a "10" at home? This reveals what's in the heart of man—his deep dissatisfaction of soul. Beauty isn't enough to fill it.

We all do it. We trade spouses, jobs, churches, friends, homes, cars, computers, and furniture for the latest and best model. There is and will always be something out there that looks better to us than what we have, unless we learn to place our value on something more lasting.

External beauty isn't all that compelling by itself anyhow. Many beautiful people are at a disadvantage for finding happiness because they can be self-centered and narcissistic. I have met some incredibly beautiful people in my life that I wouldn't want to be stuck on an elevator with for three minutes. Beauty is only skin-deep and won't bridge incompatibility or maintain a relationship. There has to be something deeper, a connection of two people based upon that which is unfading by time and age.

The other problem with placing too much value on appearances is that we are not given a choice about what we look like, so why do we reward or penalize people for that? Our appearance is just an arrangement of genes that our parents handed down to us and has no bearing on our essence or character. To make a judgment about anything based on appearances is so faulty, yet we do it every day of our lives. I admit that I am guilty as much as the next person.

In his great love for us, God wants to heal us of this futile way of thinking. If we can grasp our infinite worth as children of the Divine, we will realize that rejection ("sin") has no merit. God made us perfectly in His (and Her) image.

Laughter: Still the Best Medicine

Steve and I decided we might as well make the best of our situation until I went home, so we went ahead with the plans we had for the weekend, which included skiing the next day. I was inwardly panicking because I had only been skiing a couple times—both with disastrous results—but I wasn't about to admit it. I did wonder if I should stop to purchase a life insurance policy before we headed up the mountain, but I thought he might get a little suspicious.

I had so completely given up the difficult situation of the night before to God; I was able to enjoy myself. We spent the day together comfortably, like old friends. Thankfully, I had been on a rigorous weight lifting program and was able to keep up the pace with the "international ski model" for the whole day. I knew he was secretly impressed with my endurance and athletic ability when he asked me in the middle of the afternoon, "Think you're ready to try something a little more challenging than the parking lot now?"

Skiing went better than I thought it would, and I didn't break anything—unless you count the chairlift employee's shin I hit with my ski while getting on. However, I did practically get frostbite on my feet. The last four times down the mountain I

Filling in the Middle

kept complaining about my feet being cold, but his were fine so he thought I was being a wimp. He kept saying, "They can't be *that* cold. Let's just take one more run before we go in for some hot chocolate." By the time we got in, my feet didn't feel cold anymore.

After helping me take off my boots in the toasty ski lodge, Steve felt my toes and bellowed, "Your feet feel like ice! How long have they been this way? Why didn't you tell me?" Work with me here...can men be aggravating or what? Another twenty minutes of skiing and it would have required a complete amputation. I did find out why his feet stayed nice and warm. Come to find out later, he had electric boot heaters (years after writing this book, I still give him a bad time about that).

Finally back at the house that night, Steve lit a cozy fire after dinner so that we could shake the chill from the day. After the dishes were done, Terry and Sandi retired for the evening to their second floor hide-away. I was getting relaxed on the couch when Steve pulled out a book he had purchased before the weekend to surprise me. At the time I thought it was a sweet gesture, but had I thought about it a little more, I probably should have been offended.

The name of the book was something like, "The Absolute Quickest Way to Change Your Child." Like maybe he was suggesting something to me about my kids. When I came to my senses and asked him about it later, he swore he wasn't insinuating anything about my children; he just wanted to make an effort to encourage me as a parent.

Sitting back into the leather couch by the fireplace, we began to read the book that bore such a compelling title. It was a very small book of only about six or seven short chapters and promised in the introduction to be a condensed must-have handbook on successful parenting. In fact, the author stated right up front that he would waste no time in getting to the point. That's exactly the kind of book parents of busy young children like: short, to the point, and life changing. It was sure to be a remarkable read.

The Perfect Fit

We read the first chapter. Pretty introductory. Okay, now we must be coming up to the really good stuff.

We read the second chapter. Still introductory. Not sure where the author is going yet, but trying to keep an open mind here. Must be time to really dive into the life changing parenting skills promised by the title.

Before Steve got very far into the third chapter, the realization hit me. What began as chuckles turned into loud cackles. When I doubled over onto the floor, Steve finally caught on and he got in on the hysteria. Pretty soon we were both rolling on the floor, hooting and snorting, gasping for air, tears streaming down our cheeks. We were unable to even speak a word to each other for at least twenty minutes because, every time we tried to gain composure, another wave of hysteria hit. It was truly the best abs workout I'd had in weeks!

We'd read three whole chapters (almost half of the book) and hadn't even gotten one usable tip on how to be a better parent. We even went back after our initial gut-burst and skimmed over the remaining chapters to see if the guy was ever going to make a point or not, and we never found one, which made us start up all over again. We decided that whoever wrote the book must have been in the midst of a mental breakdown—probably from parenting. If you need good laugh once in awhile, this book truly is a must have for your personal library! It may not have helped me as a parent, but it sure brought some good laughter into my life on a night when I needed it.

Nothing but the Truth

Despite some of the obstacles it brings, being truthful is crucial in a healthy relationship and I truly wanted it to be the foundation of our friendship. As you know, I already had to admit difficult things to Steve the night of the "opal episode," but God still had to skim off another one of my glaring character struggles that floated to the surface during the weekend.

Before meeting Steve, I had allowed some dishonest defense mechanisms to take root in my life. This was partly due to the

Filling in the Middle

lack of grace and even punishing attitudes I received when admitting my mistakes to prominent people in my life. I had learned that, sometimes lying was easier than telling the truth if I thought I was going to get "beat up" for the truth. At that time, I didn't have the self-confidence to live fully in my skin and not care what people thought.

I was conscious of this struggle in my parenting and didn't want my children to suffer at home for telling the truth. We had an often-reinforced policy that anytime they told the truth, they would not be punished. On the contrary, if they lied and I found out about it, they would receive double punishment. I knew that being rewarded for honesty will not always be the experience for them in the world, but I wanted to encourage honesty as much as possible in their young lives by taking away their fear of punishment.

The very next morning, Steve had his first run-in with my unusually high fear of unpleasant consequences. It was so absurd; it was yet another sitcom in the making. After a pancake breakfast, Steve went into the bathroom to brush his teeth. A few moments later he popped his head out of the bathroom, and with an accusatory tone in his voice he said, "Did you use my toothpaste?"

Whoa. He looks upset. Maybe he's a germophobe or obsessive about people using his toothpaste and if I say yes, he's going to take me out and plunge my head into a snow bank. Maybe he will humiliate me in front of Terry and Sandi like a criminal. A dozen irrational fears crowded into one second.

"No, why would I use your toothpaste?" I masked my fear with a feeble smile. Luckily he let the conversation drop and went back to brushing his teeth.

He probably didn't mean it as accusingly as it sounded, but I don't know who else in the world would actually notice that someone had used their toothpaste and then go to the trouble to ask about it. You'd think I'd borrowed his underwear! But regardless of the irrationality of it all, I reacted out of fear. Even though it was so insignificant, I was plagued with guilt about this whole toothpaste incident, because I *had* used his toothpaste. But it was just a little lie—what difference would it make in the long run if I lied about a dab of toothpaste? Sheesh!

I realize that I'm making Steve sound like a jerk at times, but don't forget—this is my story and I'm telling it from my perspective. If he was telling his side, or if you knew the equally bizarre things I probably did to him, you would get a whole different picture. But for now, I want your sympathy and emotional support, so we're going to focus on Steve's problematic behaviors.

At the end of those four weeks—oops, I mean four days—pretending to enjoy myself, we loaded up our stuff for the drive back down the mountain to Denver, where I would catch my plane home. It would be such a relief to escape to the sanctuary of my home where I could lick my wounds in privacy. Then I would pick up the pieces and go on as before, with at least the benefit of some new standards for a future mate, and some improving character qualities in myself.

As we said our farewells to our hosts, Terry took my hand in his and said in front of Steve, "It was nice to finally meet the female version of Steve."

Steve and I looked at each other with wonder. Although we were unaware of our personality similarities, they apparently impressed upon Terry. One could not mistake the awkward moment that followed, probably making Steve feel insulted as he was brought down a few notches to my level. After all, he had mentioned being an international ski model to me at least eight times that weekend—enough to make me want to impale myself on a ski pole. I had an overwhelming temptation at that very moment to mention to him that my parents almost named me Stephanie.

A Contradictory Conclusion

Taking in the mountain scenery aglow in the low winter sun, I focused on the inspirational music coming from the stereo. I was finally on my way home. It was settled in my heart: I didn't need a man to be happy. I had so many blessing in my life,

Filling in the Middle

including my two sweet daughters waiting for me to get home. I was glad I met Steve. I had learned a lot from our friendship. Life was good.

"I had fun this weekend. Thanks for coming up." Steve's words broke into my thoughts.

"Sure. Thanks for teaching me to ski—and for everything else."

"I have so much fun when we're together. I've never had a friend like you before."

"You mean a friend that can cut hair or one that lives in Wyoming?" *Or that is painful to look at? Or that lies about using your toothpaste?* I was trying to get him to be more specific.

"I feel so comfortable when we're together. I feel like I can talk to you about anything and you understand. You know," he grabbed a handful of sunflower seeds and popped them in his mouth, "I don't think anyone laughs at my jokes like you do."

"Maybe that's because they're not that funny and I'm the only polite person you know."

"God is so awesome!" He ignored my teasing insult. "I can't believe how He provided a plane ticket for you this weekend."

"I agree. I was amazed how easily it all worked out."

"Julie...I...I'm sorry about the other night. I don't understand what's going on in my head. I have all of these conflicting feelings. I know some of the things I said must be...hurtful."

Not much more hurtful than sawing my arm off with a dull butter knife! I wanted to shout. Instead I just smiled sweetly and nodded my head.

"Hey," he looked over at me with a tender expression. "I just want you to know...I think you are really beautiful. Those feelings I am having don't mean that I don't. It's more of a problem with what I envisioned for myself. I don't want you to feel bad about yourself. You are really pretty."

"Then your stomach doesn't turn when you look at me, like you made it sound the other night? I mean, that's how it came across."

Pain flashed across his face. "I'm sorry, Julie. I'm not very good at expressing things sometimes. I really mean it...that I

The Perfect Fit

think you are an attractive woman. I wish we could start over with that conversation. Seems like I've gotten myself into trouble before for not thinking before I speak." We both laughed at his reminder of our first letter confrontation.

"You know Steve; one thing I like about you is that you are true to your feelings. I know you were obviously really burdened the other night or you wouldn't have spoken out like you did. I guess it's good that we can be honest with each other, even if it hurts sometimes. It's better than storing up all that junk and then hurting each other more later. We all need to be able to be more honest—like you have been. I want to thank you that you thought you could trust me with those candid thoughts." I had come a long way in those few days. I really meant what I was saying to him.

"Really? That is amazing you can say that. There aren't many women who could be that strong under the circumstances."

"Don't give me the credit. I'm not that strong without help."

"I love the way you rely on God so much. That is such a beautiful trait in a woman." *A beautiful trait. Christ's strength and light in me, shining out.* Eyes were being opened.

After a few moments of comfortable silence, he said, "Would you like to see a movie in Denver before we head back to the airport? We've got time."

"Sure, that sounds great."

The remaining part of the day we joked and relaxed like old buddies. There wasn't a hint of the holding back that I sensed throughout the weekend. He seemed genuinely happy and content. Forgetting the previous tension, it seemed as if we didn't have a care in the world. As we arrived in Denver, we stopped to see, "You've Got Mail," an appropriate romantic comedy that started on the Internet.

Finally, after a quick dinner of fried rice and egg rolls, we realized that it was time to get me to the airport or I would be stuck in Denver for another day. Saying goodbye at the terminal, I expressed my appreciation for the weekend; pretty sure I wouldn't be seeing him anymore. I fought off sad feelings as I left him standing on the concourse, letting him go. I still

Filling in the Middle

believed that, warts and all, Stephen Ferwerda was an incredible guy, and I couldn't imagine the girl that would capture his heart. But it wouldn't be me—that was sure.

As you probably know by now, God delights in the odds. With man, many things are impossible. But with God, all things are possible. The plans we make and achieve seem ordinary and often uninspiring. The dreams God makes and achieves through us are superhuman, bigger than we can think or imagine. Only God knew whether anything could ever work out between Steve and me someday, but it would surely take a miracle.

All I know is that when I got home—an hour and a half later, I had an email and a phone message waiting for me.

"Julie, this is Steve. I really had fun this weekend and, well...I miss you already. I wish you were still here. I can't wait to see you again. Call me when you get home. Bye." After all he put me through over the weekend *he couldn't wait to see me again*? I had given up on our relationship, trying to put it all behind me, and now this? And guys say we girls are fickle and indecisive! *Whatever!*

I was being so cautious with my feelings, praying frequently for divine guidance and direction. I wasn't feeling any particular discouragement in my heart, so we continued to communicate by phone and email. I waited patiently to see where all this was going while setting up a necessary emotional distance from Steve. I kept my heart as neutral as a gal possibly can when she has been spending time with the most incredible guy and annoying international ski model she has ever met.

Life is a series of moments, each one important to the finished picture, yet none of them independently defining. Some of them are more apparently significant, accentuating marks in the finished picture. One such moment was just around the corner. Ah yes, the moment that was so brief, so unexpected, yet monumental enough to change my world.

The Perfect Fit

Stand on the Sidelines
(Let Go of the Need to Control)

Three weeks after the disastrous ski weekend, Steve and I had an opportunity to see each other again on my way through Denver airport. My Mom had asked me to accompany her to visit some friends in San Diego, the perfect chance for a little mid-winter reprieve. Since our eventful weekend, Steve had been sweeter and more attentive than ever. I still had a great peace about everything, so I decided to go along with the unpredictable friendship for a while and see what happened. During my week-long trip, Steve called me every day to chat, but there were still plenty of juicy details to discuss over dinner in the ultra-modern Denver airport.

Throughout our brief visit, I couldn't help noticing that Steve carried a little pink gift bag around with him as comfortably as if it was one of his new fashion accessories.

It must be something for me. He must have really missed me if he actually bought me a gift this week! Although I was curious, I pretended not to notice, waiting for him to bring it up.

After a couple of lively hours, Steve walked us to the gate where the tiny prop plane, not much bigger than a mosquito hawk, awaited. Pushing the last bite of dripping mint chocolate chip waffle cone into his mouth, Steve finally placed the pink bag into my eager hands.

"Don't open it until you get on the plane—it's an early Valentine's gift."

"Will it bite?"

"Only if you try to open it before you're airborne." His eyes sparkled with mischief.

"Hey, thanks for taking the time to meet us. You were sweet to do all of this...I can't wait to see what's in here."

Reaching out for me, his warm hug goodbye was heavy and lingering. With a smile and a wave we were whisked out into the bitter cold January night, where our plane waited fifty yards away from the terminal.

Filling in the Middle

Several minutes later in the semi-dark plane, his tender words and expression replayed in my mind. I was almost afraid to open that bag because I didn't want the moment to pass. I love savoring surprises, and thought about saving it until I got home. However, I'm also as curious as a cat staring down a moving target, and it's not every day you get a pink mystery bag from an international ski model! Unable to stand the suspense; I had to know what was in that bag.

Slowly and carefully unwinding the ribbon, I reached into the bag to discover a host of little surprises tucked inside—some of them curiously random and others decidedly sentimental. Starting at the top I pulled out a deck of cards from his jigsaw puzzle company, a little pocket guide for dream interpretation—a joke to help me interpret my bizarre dreams, some candy, some music by one of his favorite artists, an early Valentine's Day card, some Grandma's cookies (definitely a bonus move), and our movie ticket stubs from *You've Got Mail* as a memoir. After emptying the bulk of the contents, I looked inside to see if I missed anything and...oh, wait! What's this? Daisies taken off their stems and some rose petals...the bottom was covered in white rose petals.

It took a moment for the implications to sink in. But then it hit me. *White rose petals come from...white roses!* Brilliant deduction, I know. But it was a moment I least expected, in a form I had not considered. If this was truly an answer to my prayer from over a year ago, it so caught me off guard that I almost missed it. My one-sided conversation with God after the discovery went something like this:

Is this for real? Are you kidding me? Don't play games with my head, I'm confused enough already. You wouldn't, would You? Okay, I guess the name "Steve" would cut down on some confusion. Everyone would adjust more easily and wouldn't accidentally call him by the wrong name. And He is a challenge...You know how I like a challenge, right? But how...how did you get him to agree to this? You are so sneaky! You expect me to keep this whole thing a secret?

The Perfect Fit

God had given me the confirmation I'd waited for and He did it before I invested too much time and emotional energy into this relationship. I needed to know that this was His idea, and not mine, so that I didn't feel like I was doing my own thing again. The peace and joy that flooded my heart were amazing as I thought of all the implications brought about by one little bag of rose petals. I don't think I needed an airplane to get me home that night. I was flying already.

In order to not put any premature expectations on Steve before God had a chance to bring him to the same conclusion, I determined not to tell Steve the white rose story until the day that he asked me to marry him. It was important for Steve to hear God tell him, not me. Personally, I resent other people boxing me in with a "word from God" about me that He hasn't spoken to me yet—it is so manipulative. Pepe Le Pew had already tried that trick—telling me that God told him I was going to be his wife. Ugh! You might as well lead me around with a dog collar. Besides, how did he know it was *God's* voice? And if it was really God, why didn't He tell *me*?

If God wasn't big enough to let Steve in on the secret without my help, then we might as well scrap the whole thing. Just because God had let me in on the plan at this point in time didn't mean that everyone was privy simultaneously. The Story must play out at the pace of the Writer. It mustn't be rushed or ordered by me, a casted character. Besides, I was just learning how much fun it is to have secrets with God. God, the Creator of the Universe, trusted me with a secret. That awareness was more exciting than any secret in and of itself!

As soon as I got home I called Steve to thank him for the thoughtful and sweet gifts. You don't have to guess that I also had ulterior motives. True to my female nature, I wanted details! Carefully and with the nonchalance of a skilled detective, I asked the critical questions. "So...those white rose petals were so creative, why did you buy white roses?"

"Well, if you must know, I was walking around the fresh flower section of Freddy's Flowers and Gifts, trying to find something really special and meaningful for your gift bag, when

Filling in the Middle

I felt a sudden compelling urge—like this irresistible magnetic force—just drawing me over to the white roses. I just knew there must be a special significance so I had to get them for you. Are white roses your favorite or something?"

Snapped back to reality from my sappy daydream, his real answer was much less inspiring. "I dunno. I think they were on sale." His answer suddenly brought me down a notch. Is it possible the white rose petals were just a coincidence? Was I reading too much into this? Maintaining my cautious optimism I realized whether Steve had any idea or not why he bought the roses, he still picked white. No man had ever bought me white roses before. With just enough mystery in the equation to keep things exciting, only time would tell me the answers I wanted to know.

> "What is faith? It is the confident assurance that what we hope for is going to happen. It is the evidence of things we cannot yet see." Hebrews 11:1 (NLT)

Crest on the Conscience

I've never felt guilty before about using toothpaste, but as the days and weeks wore on, so did my nagging conscience. I thought it was insane to be still rehashing guilt over lying about using Steve's toothpaste, but my conscience wouldn't give it a rest. It was driving me crazy that I hadn't told him the truth. I needed to clear the air. It was time to squeeze out the contents of the tube, so to speak. In great humiliation and embarrassment I finally blurted it out one day on the phone.

"Steve, I *did* use your toothpaste *and* I lied about it. I'm sorry."

"Aha! *I knew it!*" he declared smugly. Most people would have drawn a blank if you brought up something as insignificant as using their toothpaste a month ago and would have said, "Huh? What toothpaste? I don't know what you're talking about." But not Steve! He knew the instant it left my mouth exactly what I was referring to. But now I was free. My conscience could finally rest in peace.

The Perfect Fit

Attraction Distraction

The next five months had one common thread—the testing of my faith in what I believed God had spoken to me. There was apparently a big obstacle in our way, because it kept resurfacing. *That attraction thing again.*

Anything worth having in life is going to be tested and frequently face bleak moments and obstacles. This is a great opportunity to practice patience, growth, and not getting too attached to outcomes lest our motives become tainted. It's also important to keep our hope and meaning in God at difficult times. The last thing I needed to do was to start putting my hope in Steve Ferwerda. Regardless of whether this relationship went the way I wanted it to or not, I could not let my faith in God waiver. I had to keep reminding myself that God did not want me to be unhappy or miserable, and that He was committed to a plan of good for my life. All He wanted me to do was take one day at a time and love Him wholeheartedly.

I consulted no one about the rose promise or the rose petals, because I still didn't know what God was doing exactly. Things could take all sorts of strange twists and turns. I wasn't going to chance getting ahead of God's timing, or look foolish if I misinterpreted something. Trusting God somewhat blindly, without the aid of a person validating my interpretations or urging me to stand solid on what God had told me was a big test. It was just me and God again. No one could help me with my doubts or questions; no person could soothe my inner struggles and insecurities. And certainly no one else could help me with the obstacles that were lurking around the corner. It was time to be patient and wait to see how it all played out.

Try not to jump to any conclusions and time will tell. If this is really God telling me Steve is to be my husband, I will see the fruit of this promise without validation from anyone. If not, nothing will be lost. I still have God and I am content with Him alone.

Filling in the Middle

Tommy On My Doorstep

The times I was about to give up hope, special moments would come. It was as if God sent encouragement just when I needed it, as a reward for letting go of the outcome. One such moment happened on a bright Saturday afternoon in March, when I was feeling completely discouraged and rejected about Steve's discontent. Steve called me at work from Copper Mountain ski resort where he was skiing for the weekend with some friends in Colorado.

"Hey! How is my favorite Chocolate Chip Cookie Dough Girl?"

"Great! How is the skiing today?"

"Oh man, it's excellent out here today. I'm riding up the chairlift right now and I just wanted to call and let you know what an awesome day I'm having while you are slaving away at work."

"That makes me feel a lot better. When are you guys heading home?"

"We'll probably stay until tomorrow afternoon. What are you doing this weekend?"

"I was thinking of going to the movie tonight after work. Then tomorrow there's a potluck after church and the girls and I are always up for that! Those church ladies sure can cook!"

"Sounds good. I could use a home-cooked meal myself. I've been solo this week while Terry and Sandi stayed up in the mountains."

"You poor thing. You'll have to find your own potluck. Don't they have a church potluck directory down there in Denver...so bachelors can find out which church to visit each Sunday?"

"If not they should get one! Are you going to the movie with, Vicky?" He tried to sound jealous, but I knew he was having more fun engaged in his favorite sport.

"No, I'm going by myself. Vicky has a meeting tonight."

"So what time are you going to be home? I'll give you a call later."

"I'll probably be home by nine o'clock. If not, I'll call you when I get home."

"Okay. Well, I'll talk to you then. Bye."

The Perfect Fit

"Thanks for calling, talk to you later."

After a couple more hours of work, I grabbed a bite to eat and headed to the movie theatre. Afterward, when I arrived home, I was surprised by a beautiful bouquet of purple chrysanthemums sitting on my front doorstep. Following my nose, I located a business card stuck down in the leaves that was literally swimming in men's "Tommy" cologne.

That's strange. Only Steve knew I liked Tommy cologne. And whose business card was this? A certain Denver department store that Steve and I had visited together on one of my recent trips down to see him was the only information on the card. No more clues. No note, no writing at all. Just the card and Tommy, alone on my doorstep, inside a bouquet of mums.

As usual, my mind was going in high-speed circles, trying to solve the mystery. The flowers had to be from Steve because he was the only one who knew about Tommy, and the business card was from the same store we visited in Denver. But how did he get this gift to Riverton? He was skiing in Copper, at least five hours away. *Maybe he sent it up with someone. No, that would be too much trouble.*

As soon as I got in the door, the neighbors began calling. Apparently the whole neighborhood could smell the bouquet, which was so immersed in cologne that it soon wilted.

Setting my new aromatic bouquet on the dining room table, I knew that however he arranged for them to get delivered, it had taken very special planning. Missing him, and touched by this sweet and romantic gesture, I wished I could thank him in person. While waiting for him to call me from Colorado to explain the mystery, there was a knock at the door. Probably one of my neighbors coming over to stick their nose in my flowers—I mean my business. This night was getting pretty strange.

Not sure what to expect when I opened the door, my dreams came true! It was a Girl Scout cookie salesman! Okay, I made that up. Unfortunately, it was too late for cookies, but the visitor was the next best thing to cookies—Steve Ferwerda! Hugging him tightly, I squealed, "What in the world are you

Filling in the Middle

doing here? You couldn't stand to miss out on that potluck, could you?"

I couldn't believe he drove all that way since we'd talked just hours before. He had to have given up half a day of skiing just to surprise me! They say love makes you do irrational things, but I thought it was especially crazy because it was already Saturday night and I thought he would have to leave early the next day to get back to Denver. Later he explained that he didn't have to be to work until the middle of the week because he was using some vacation days.

With every gallant tale, the hero must overcome opposition while trying to win over the princess, usually bearing a battle scar to attest to his bravery. This evening was no exception. Holding out his bleeding hand, Steve explained that while he was spraying the bottle of Tommy cologne on the card and flowers in the dark car, he accidentally cut himself on the lid. Princess Julie was on the scene right away, bandaging him up in no time. However, judging from the scar that was left behind, the matter probably warranted professional attention. It remains to this day as a tribute to his gallant feat.

Building a Case

Although Steve and I were very close friends, talking on the phone daily, writing meaningful letters, seeing each other at every opportunity, we were still not "romantically" involved by today's standards. I was very glad of this because it helped me to maintain sanity and objectivity each time I felt rejected. Over and over in the ensuing months he cycled through not being overly attracted to the outer me, yet conflicted because of his growing feelings for the inner me. It was a case of a heart at war with a mind. One minute he could not imagine his life without me, the next he was not sure he wanted me.

Ever ready to insert humor into the story at the appropriate places, God began to have some fun with Steve's struggle. It seemed that every single time that he admitted his struggle to me; God arranged for someone to approach Steve in front of me—usually the same day—to give him a different perspective.

The Perfect Fit

His friends and family expressed things to him like: *"Your gal is hot—what does she see in you? ...How did you get so lucky? ...You're really dating up these days!"* After the third or fourth time, it became pretty hilarious, even to Steve. Of course, in light of spiritual matters, beauty is only skin deep and didn't make him "lucky" to have me, but it felt like God was behind those affirmations, and perhaps they were more about bolstering my fragile self-esteem than influencing Steve.

Part of Steve's inner conflict came from the fact that he was thirty-two years old and had never even been close to making a marriage commitment to someone. Thinking about walking through such an important door of no return brought about an expected fear of finality. He was afraid that there was still something better out there for him and he might miss it if he got tied down. As much as anyone, I knew how that lie worked, but I couldn't help him through it. During this time, I had come to believe that I was the one that God was setting before Steve as His best offering. And though Steve wondered waffled about the potential options, there wouldn't be another woman in the whole world that would be a better match for him if God was leading him to marry me.

God, what if Steve doesn't want Your best for him? What if he chooses, based upon his sight and misplaced desires? I mean, sight is a powerful, tangible thing. What will give him the strength to choose what is more lasting? Help Steve to choose Your will and Your best for his life. Help Steve to be willing for You to change his heart.

Waiting in silence day-by-day, month-by-month to see where all this was going to end up took incredible patience and courage. There was nothing I could do to help things along. I constantly had to resist the urge to control the outcome, and just wait quietly while God did His work.

Would Steve trust God's plan for his future, believing that God's will is the best and most joyful path for his life? I didn't know what was ahead, but most days it still looked impossible.

Filling in the Middle

Red Light—Green Light
(Pay Attention to Signs)

Getting to my hometown would be impossible without the right tools. Navigating to our remote location requires that you study maps and road signs carefully and frequently to make sure you stay on the right track. Arriving at your divinely appointed destination is no different. You must rely on your inner navigation system and study the signs frequently to keep from getting sidetracked.

I knew that if Steve and I were supposed to be together, I would have to encounter one particular road sign along the way. God was going to have to do something about Steve's family. Now don't get me wrong, there was nothing wrong with his family—that was the problem. Although it was extremely important to me that I marry someone with a family that loved and accepted me as one of their own, I doubted that I could ever fit in with Steve's family. A conservative missionary family, things were intimidatingly unblemished from all appearances.

After growing up on the mission field, Steve and his three siblings attended Wheaton College, a noted conservative Christian college. His sister stayed in the Middle East to pursue full time mission work with her husband. Everything about his family—from the gene pool right down to how they conducted their outward lives—emitted signals of conservative, upright, and moral. How could a family like that ever possibly accept me in light of my gene pool, divorce, mistakes, and embarrassing cookie addiction? I didn't want to enter a marriage where I felt rejection or tension over my past, or where I never felt like I was up to a standard, or be living in any kind of tension with the in-laws. I also didn't want to feel like he was going against his family's wishes by choosing me for a wife, as that would be extremely isolating and difficult for both of us.

God this is all in Your hands. It looks precarious. If this relationship is your idea, unlock doors and make room for me in the hearts of Steve's family.

The Perfect Fit

A Letter of Acceptance

In January I wrote letters to Steve's family. This was a very difficult step, because both Steve and I felt that, in order for his family to have a fair chance to accept me, they needed to know what and whom they were accepting. After a couple letters of general correspondence, we wrote an honest letter to them together, letting them know all about me. This included the details of my past and present, and my wholehearted love for God and desire to follow His will for my life. I also let them know how special Steve was becoming to me. We sent it off by email and waited impatiently as several days went by with no response. I imagined the worst.

After a week of nerve-wracking anticipation, we heard back. Steve's sister, Ruth Anne, wrote first to tell us that Steve's mom was declining rapidly in her health, and that is why it had taken so long for them to get back to us. Steve's mom had been battling cancer for thirty years, and it was suddenly getting the best of her. She had fought so long and hard to hold on to life, that it didn't seem possible she was in her dying days.

After informing us of Steve's mom's extremely ill and weakened condition, Steve's sister typed out her handwritten letter of response, dated January 29, 1999, and emailed it to me. Marian had insisted that she be the one to write this letter to me, laboring carefully and painstakingly. Since she had been too ill and weak to hand write any other letters for several weeks, Ruth Anne pointed out how special that letter was.

In beautiful, graceful words, she assured me that she accepted me and was happy about my friendship with her son. Her warm and loving tone throughout the letter brought tears to my eyes. Near the bottom of the letter, I was stopped by an unclear blessing of some sort. "I see that God is giving you the desires of your heart, just like He did for me." What did she mean by this sentence? The expression clearly had meaning as did every other intentional word of her letter, but it was undecipherable to me. Hopefully, I would be able to ask her soon what she meant.

Filling in the Middle

I didn't get the chance. Five days later, on February 3, 1999—my oldest daughter's eighth birthday—Marian Ferwerda passed from this world. Her letter to me was the very last one she wrote on this earth, making it all the more special to me.

Even though I didn't know this woman, I could see her wonderful qualities through her son. He often told me stories of the many times they made special memories together when he was a child. They went fishing, cooked in the kitchen, went for frequent walks, and did many other things together. He told me what an incredible teacher and patient mother she'd been. I could see all these qualities shining through, and I admired her all the more.

Any family barriers that may have existed came down in miraculous unity. Not only did I get the assurance from his mom before she died that I was welcome into her heart in whatever capacity God placed me in her son's life, but generally the rest of the family responded the same toward me. I think that even Steve was surprised by the response of his family. It was definitely a miracle that we couldn't ignore in considering a future together.

Moving Right Along

Late February, Steve and I began praying together about taking another step in our deepening friendship. We felt like we needed more focused time together to figure out if we should move forward. We did our best to stay objective by keeping romantic expressions at bay and waiting on God for direction, but we felt like we needed daily time together before seriously considering a long-term commitment. We were both cautious, knowing how people can appear to be one thing at a distance, but when you live close enough to see them every day, the warts show up. Granted, we both could see some warts already, but were there deal-breakers yet undiscovered?

About this time, an employment door opened. It wasn't exactly a lateral career move and didn't even look like a sensible option, but it was an opportunity and Steve was ready for an excuse to leave the rat race of Denver. He figured he could take

The Perfect Fit

this job, and if things worked out between us, he could look for a better, more gratifying and suitable job. If things didn't work out, he could move on to a location where he'd rather be.

He negotiated starting the job the first week of April to give him time to wrap up obligations in Denver with his current employer. He also needed to make the preparations necessary to sell his puzzle company—something he was planning to do soon as well. In spite of Steve's yo-yo emotions about our relationship, my confidence was growing little by little that I did indeed hear God right by how things were unfolding and prayers were being answered.

A huge boost of confidence came in March, just before Steve moved to Riverton. He had barely started thinking about selling his successful puzzle business when an interested buyer contacted him out of the blue! The puzzle business, which catered to Colorado ski resorts, had become a huge undertaking for one person. The thought of trying to run it from out of state was daunting. The buyer, who had practically appeared out of nowhere, named a fair price for the business upfront. I could almost read the headlines from this divinely orchestrated development. "Master Pieces Together Yet Another Puzzler."

When the Chips Were Down

A couple weeks before Steve moved to my hometown in Riverton, Wyoming, it was my birthday. As a special surprise, he purchased two "Family Life" Conference tickets for us in Denver. This conference for married couples and those considering marriage focused on spiritual growth in a relationship, good communication, and dealing with conflict. Steve thought it would be good for us to attend so that we might get more insight about the direction of our relationship and our compatibility. It would also be a good opportunity before he moved to Riverton for us to work through more issues and to have some bonding time together.

When I arrived for the weekend pulling a utility trailer to bring a load of his things back to Riverton, there was a difference in the air. A new line had been crossed; a new frontier

Filling in the Middle

waited to be explored. The excitement and anticipation hung between us with the knowledge that in just two short weeks, Steve would make his big move to the "Western Outback."

Planning a relationship enrichment weekend for us was one of the best birthday presents Steve could have thought of. The speakers, consisting of husband and wife teams, were very humorous, insightful, and vulnerable. One speaker focused on that all-important character trait of humility when dealing with conflicts that arise in marriage. His presentation was so motivating that I was ready to apologize to Steve ahead of time for future conflict.

During his talk, he inserted a humorous story about an ill-fated canary "Chippy." Chippy, the speaker told us, was a canary famously adored and admired by all who listened to his beautiful song. After the events of one fateful day, however, things got down and dirty for Chippy.

It all started when Chippy's owner was vacuuming and accidentally sucked Chippy up the long hose and into the vacuum bag. Frantically, she turned off the giant dirt tunnel, opened up the nasty bag, and dug through dirt, carpet fibers, crumbs, hair and whatever else was in there, to rescue Chippy. Somehow the delicate bird had lived, in spite of impossible odds.

The woman hurriedly took the unrecognizable little dust ball into the bathroom and ran him under the faucet to clean him up. Seeing the poor, shivering mass of soggy feathers, she worried about Chippy catching cold, so she whipped out her hairdryer and blow-dried the bird into a big fluffy ball. Placing him back in his cage, she hoped he would successfully recover from the ordeal. The speaker then delivered the clincher: Chippy was so traumatized that...he never sang again! Not one chirp.

The speaker told this story for some comic relief, and indeed it was funny. But what was even funnier to Steve and me is that we had both heard this story before and knew that the bird's name was really "*Chirpy*." Without the right name, the story practically misses the point. Chirpy got his impressive name and status because of his beautiful, delightful song. I mean, what good is it that "Chippy" didn't sing anymore? But, with a name like "*Chirpy*," now that tells you something about the bird's song prowess.

Thinking the speaker would be ever so grateful if we let him in on the misinformation; we decided to approach him after his presentation. That way, when he told this story in the future, it would make the intended point more effectively. Besides, our willingness to correct his story would give our speaker an opportunity to demonstrate, by example, his lifestyle of humility to his attentive students.

Finding him at one of the breaks, we gently and graciously relayed the true name of our feathered friend. Would you believe that when we told him, he didn't seem to appreciate our help at all? Perhaps it was embarrassment or, God forbid, maybe pride, but he gave an obligatory half smile and turned away to fill up his glass of water on the table behind him, dismissing us. I guess there's a difference between humility and humiliation.

Consider the Source

With the reality of the big move drawing near, the impact of the changes began to sink in for Steve and me. Was I ready for this? Was he ready for this? Occasionally, disturbing questions invaded my thoughts and cast serious doubts about what was in store.

Even if I do marry a man who loves You, God, there are no guarantees, right? I mean what if I marry Steve, being absolutely certain today that he loves You, believing You brought us together, and a few years down the road he walks away, claiming things have changed and that he doesn't love me anymore? I would rather stay single than go through that heartache again. If Steve is Your man for me, how do I know he won't throw away his vows when he gets bored or tired of me, or thinks he's missing out on something better? What assurance can You give me?

I felt the familiar peace that accompanies the moments God speaks into my heart. Though not audible, these were my impressions of His reply: "I'm glad you asked, Julie. It is safe to

Filling in the Middle

trust your heart to My provision. When people try to love with their own human love, it often falls short because it is imperfect and incomplete. But if I lead you into marriage again, I will choose a man who will always be devoted to the principles of divine love. My unfailing, unconditional love will be poured into his heart for you. It will never run dry or fall short."

Joy flooded my heart as I imagined that kind of love, pouring from the very heart of God through the man He chose for me, overflowing into my heart. I would be the guaranteed recipient of that love, originating from my Heavenly Father's heart.

I tried to visualize what this might look like in the natural world and found the imagery while sitting in front of my south-facing window one cold winter's day. The sun shone through the window, warming me in its rays. The source of the warm penetrating light was the sun, and I was the object of its light and warmth, transmitted to me by the clear glass window. In the same way, God is the source of love; my future husband would be the window that God's love shone through, bringing light and warmth into my life. The very thought of it was thrilling!

In the same way, you and I are the targets of God's compassion and love. His love is everlasting, unfailing, and complete. I believe the only way a person can love another so completely is if they love with God's love. God made a covenant with me that day that His choice of a husband would be that window allowing His constant stream of love to shine through.

A Week with Bill

Two weeks later, Steve pulled into my driveway with the rest of his earthly belongings. It would be the understatement to say that Steve was having second thoughts the week he gave up his secure promising job in Denver to move to a dinky little backwoods town without so much as a high-speed Internet connection (thankfully, that all changed in the course of time). We did have one major intersection in town—what more do you need when you have more cows than people? It never takes me more than seven minutes to get all the way across town to work,

The Perfect Fit

even when following a senior citizen. The crime gets bad in the summer though. You just never know what one of those pesky raccoons is going to steal next out of your yard. I would trade the rat race of city life, high crime, and heavy traffic jams any day for this!

At least Steve waited until the second day to show his culture shock. He did a great "Bill the cat" impression, the look of terror-struck frenzy written across his entire body. The worst was his hypnotic-like monotone announcement at least every two hours, "If things don't work out here, I can always move away." After two weeks of this, I was ready to scream, *"If I hear that one more time I'm going to beg Pepe Le Pew to come back!"* It's confusing to me why mercy never shows up on tests as one of my spiritual gifts.

While Steve was having his meltdown, seemingly on the verge of making an escape, I was constantly questioning God about the things I believed He had revealed to me earlier.

Did I hear You right, God? Was this relationship Your idea? Or did I want this so much, I imagined it was Your leading? If it's from You, is Steve is going to miss it? The questions played over and over in my mind. Ugh, it was so confusing!

I began second guessing everything, weighing it all out. I'm always afraid of not hearing God right by being too presumptuous. I had peace in this relationship like never before, our relationship was marked by deep respect and beautiful friendship, it was more romantic than anything I had ever experienced, and God seemed to be giving us the green light by how easily details were coming together. Still, shouldn't Steve be seeing the same road signs I was if they were more than coincidences? I had seen coincidences before. I knew how easily I could convince myself of things and get off track.

On the other hand, I didn't want to be like the Israelites or doubting Thomas, either. My constant need for reassurance was wearisome even for me and I wished I could learn once and for all how to recognize God's voice and then stand firm in His personal revelations to me, even when all the circumstances

Filling in the Middle

were not supporting His promises. This is to hope when all hope is gone. To believe what we can't see with our eyes.

Remember when the Israelites sent spies into the Promised Land and they came back with a fearful report? God had already given this land to them as their inheritance. Yet in the face of the "giant" odds, they faltered—all except for Joshua and Caleb, that is. Two men out of millions believed God and were greatly rewarded. Was I choosing belief as Joshua and Caleb, or was I giving in to the fearful report? The odds can be staggering at times, but the God of impossibilities delights in our faith, the same faith Joshua and Caleb demonstrated.

I asked God to show me what to pray and what to do next. I pleaded with Him not to lose patience with me, since my desire was to follow Him, but I just didn't trust myself. As I prayed, a peace once again fell over me, quieting my restless heart. I felt as if God whispered to my heart, "Be patient, this is normal behavior for a guy who's just given up his job, way of life, and many of his dreams to follow a girl living in the middle of nowhere with two kids, a past, and brown hair. The poor guy doesn't even know what is going on here yet. Just give him a little time and space to adjust before you panic. Oh, and Julie...have you checked out the grocery sales on ice cream this week?"

They do say the way to a man's heart is through his stomach.

Sex: Now or Later?
(Think it Through)

Even though Steve and I are adults, we had the same set of difficult decision to make regarding how to handle intimacy in our relationship. Steve was a thirty-two year old virgin, and I felt it was important to demonstrate to him that I could be trusted to be faithful to my marriage vows. We both felt at that stage of our lives that it was imperative we not sleep together before marriage, primarily because of our fairly rigid and conservative beliefs at that time.

But we also came to realize over time and maturity (I'm rewriting this section 20 years later) that God deals with people uniquely, and each relationship must work through this issue to the best of their ability to minimize emotional and physical wounds, as well as to facilitate the best foundation for the best future outcomes. For example, delayed gratification can be a powerful tool of pleasurable and meaningful experiences after the foundation of trust has fully been developed. But some people may be at a completely different place in their beliefs, their personalities, their backgrounds, their needs—and it is not up to me or anyone else to decide for them.

We no longer believe as we used to, that God is absolutely black and white on this issue of intimacy before marriage and that everyone must abstain from sex before marriage or be considered a moral failure under a curse of guilt or even accused of "living in sin." It was a process getting to a more moderate position for us in light of our strict background, one that resulted from many hours of looking more deeply into the intent of Scriptures, history, and our own hearts.

Having said that, sex before marriage probably isn't the best decision for everyone and should be considered carefully. Relying on physical intimacy for closeness in a relationship can be deceptive. It often gives a false, unstable foundation and clouds good judgment. No amount of physical intimacy before marriage will resolve or even improve the conflicts you will be facing during marriage. In the presence of sex during premarital dating, many elements that make up the whole person are undetected because of blinding emotion or physical excitement. We don't dig enough and get to the bottom of what we're getting ourselves into. Rather we end up getting carried along by our feelings, living for the moment.

Because the focus of typical dating relationships is usually centered on emotional expression (infatuation) and physical affection, there often not enough focus on finding out about the deep down essence of a person's core values, depth of character,

Filling in the Middle

and spiritual life. These insights cannot be determined from hearing a person's words (or any amount of coaxing); they must be silently witnesses in their lives in order to be valid. The person you are dating can tell you anything you want to hear, and you might be inclined to believe it if the relationship is more self-focused (what can I get for myself) than spiritually-focused (what does God want for me), or if you have emotional scars that impair your ability to see through flattery or insincerity, or if you are using sex as a tool to prevent rejection or tame your insecurities. The person you are dating may tell you that, after the wedding, they will focus on spiritual or deeper emotional growth together. And that promise may be enticing, but putting off the pursuit of deeper connection now may be a red flag. If it's not there now, what makes you think it will magically show up later? You don't put on and off spirituality or depth of character like a pair of work boots. It's something you are and bleeds into all areas of your life. If you don't mutually work on that connection now, it's likely you won't later, either.

Even though we have become more moderate and less judgmental on this issue, we are both still glad to this day that we waited to have sex until marriage as it provided many benefits of trust, deeper emotional intimacy, and plenty of time to work on meaningful aspects of our relationship and future together. It also gave us something really fun to look forward to, much like dreaming about cookies after Brussels sprouts!

For women who have had sex and have regrets, it's time to let go of that unproductive guilt cycle. I've been there (with my first marriage) and it's not worth rehashing things you wish you had done differently or allowing guilt of the past to cloud the now. God is not mad at you. God is bigger than that and is not petty like we often imagine. He sees your "mistakes" as necessary opportunities for your growth, so why are you holding yourself hostage to the past? I no longer believe in a "Plan B" or God doing "damage control" in our lives. Every mistake we make or regret we have is merely a necessary stop on our road to wholeness, leading to our best life now if only we can accept it and believe it. He also is not a partial parent; we are all in process of learning by trial and error the necessary beneficial lessons to guide us into a joyful, purposeful life.

It is so comforting for me to learn that all of my choices in life, good or bad, are God's "plan A" for my life, because He knows the end from the beginning, and He knows the exact price I have to pay in order to be conformed into the image of Christ. I may not choose the objectively best option the first time in a given situation, but I gain more insight, more wisdom for next time, and more empathy for others when I realize we all screw up. My wholeness matters to God more than my short-term happiness, which is why He has allowed for this path of learning through my mistakes and, at times, rebellion.* It is so freeing to know that, no matter what I choose or how I mess up, it was all a part of His plan for me from the beginning to bring about the greatest version of myself, and ultimately, my lasting happiness. Nothing is lost; everything is my teacher.

No matter what mistakes you have made, God is the God of redemption—bringing back to life what has died or been lost. He wants to mend your life. The road is not always easy, but hope and new beginnings are always available.

Purely Romance

Refraining from sexual intimacy before marriage reaped more benefits in our relationship than I could imagine. For starters, it left us with more time and energy for old-fashioned romance. There's nothing as exciting as being romanced slowly and deliberately without the pressure for sex. It builds incredibly deep feelings of being emotionally safe. It's downright fun, too!

One early spring day, Steve headed outside to mow my lawn. For what seemed like hours, I heard him out on the lawn, mowing and mowing. I wondered what was going on, since my whole lawn was only about as big as Martha Stewart's compost pile. Was he mowing the neighbor's yard by mistake? Against my infamous micro-managing inclinations, I decided against

---

* A great read on this topic is *Falling Upward: A Spirituality for the Two Halves of Life*, by Richard Rohr.

Filling in the Middle

checking up on him. Finally he came in with a cute boyish grin on his face, flushed from the cool air and rigorous exercise.

"Julie, close your eyes." He came and put an arm around me, leading me out the front door. "No peeking."

"What is it?" I giggled with anticipation.

"Just a few more steps," he slowly led me to the edge of the lawn for the right angle.

"Can I look yet?" I felt a little like Belle in *Beauty and The Beast,* when the beast was just about to reveal the massive library to her.

Steve couldn't have been any more proud than the beast when he took his hand away from my eyes to reveal the fruit of his labors worked across my whole front lawn. "Okay, open your eyes."

There in huge readable letters were the words, "I LOVE YOU" mowed into the grass. In all my life I had never seen such a sweet, romantic effort. Apparently the rest of the town hadn't either. Afterward, perfect strangers came up to me on the street, in the grocery store, at the dentist office to inquire about the big green love marquee.

Abstinence in our relationship also had a great benefit of being able to more objectively work through our many conflicts and focus on good communication. If we had been physically involved, I would have gone mad about Steve's attraction obstacle and his inability to make a commitment. As it was, I was able to enjoy my relationship with him while keeping an open hand. Well, I enjoyed most of it, that is.

Purely Romance

In May I was nearly out of patience because Steve was still unable to make up his mind about where I stood in his life. He had been in Riverton for a couple months—after the six months we had spent writing, calling, and getting together on weekends. Shouldn't he have an idea by now if I was the girl for him, especially at our ages?

The signs were all there. We were an incredible match with so many things in common. We shared our passion for God and kept our relationship focused on meaningful growth. We were definitely better together than apart. We had many of the same faults and struggles and were able to encourage each other spiritually. Through countless prayers together and apart, we both felt God's peace like never before in any relationship, assuring us that we weren't getting ahead of His leading. What was so difficult for him to figure out? After all the quality time we had spent getting to know each other over the last seven months, shouldn't it be obvious for both of us by now?

Perhaps we needed some time apart to reevaluate the situation. My Mom won a trip to Puerto Vallarta, Mexico, for outstanding sales in her insurance business, and she needed a travel companion. The timing couldn't have been more ideal, so I accepted her invitation. Packing for my trip, I felt relieved to get away for a few days. *It will be good for him to have the time he needs to figure things out while I'm away. The time apart will either help him to see the light, or he'll be ready to move on when I get back.* Although I was still convinced this relationship was God's doing, a reprieve from analyzing and wondering, not to mention a few siestas on a sunny Mexico beach, would do me a world of good. As for Steve, listening to his heart without any distractions and having some time to miss me couldn't hurt.

Frankly, I was expecting the worst. Steve's indecision made me doubt if things could work out between us—at least for now. If he wasn't willing to accept God's best provision for his life, then there would be no future for us. Believing Steve genuinely loved me, I was willing to be patient a little longer because I knew that he was confused. He showed his love in so many ways every day. I loved him, too, but I didn't know how much longer I could go through these disappointing feelings and conflicting moods of his. My best option for the moment was clear. When the going gets tough, the tough go on vacation!

A Commitment to Faithful Love

I spent the flight home from Mexico with a mix of trepidation and excitement. I was extremely curious to find out what had

Filling in the Middle

transpired in Steve's mind while we were apart. When I first saw him, it certainly didn't go the way I expected.

"I couldn't wait for you to get home. I've missed you so much." He pounced on me like a puppy in a pet store, his eyes brimming with longing and excitement.

"What a nice surprise. I missed you, too," I said, tempted to double-check to make sure I came to the right house.

"I've been so productive this week while you were away."

Taking in the newly shampooed carpet, the rearranged furniture, and some noticeable repairs, I smiled appreciatively, "I noticed! Did you happen to reupholster the furniture or drywall the garage yet?"

"Very funny. I see the tropical sun didn't interfere with your sense of humor. Hey, come down to the office. I want to show you something." He seemed more at home all the time. Grabbing a sheet of paper off the desk he pulled me over to the couch.

"Julie, this time away has been good for me. It's given me time to think about our relationship. I really can't imagine my life if I wasn't here with you now. These last few weeks have been hard with all the changes, but...it's been worth it. I'm really glad I came."

Woot! Woot! We seem to have connected a loose wire somewhere. Steve is breaking through his clouds of confusion after all. I kept silent, waiting for him to finish.

"I've written something to let you know my commitment level to you. I don't know if we will ever get married or not, but I want you to know how very special you are to me."

I began to read the loving words, written by a man who was intent upon honoring and respecting me for the duration of our friendship. *"...I pledge to keep myself pure before you and God... I want you to know that your love and respect for me is more important than a quick thrill or moment of pleasure...I will hide God's Word in my heart so that I will think about whatever is true, noble, right, pure, lovely, admirable, excellent, and praiseworthy. ...I will uphold you daily in prayer. Your Father in Heaven loves you and I love you, too..."*

The Perfect Fit

Tears spilled freely as I finished the most beautiful letter that had ever been written to me. I knew without a doubt, Steve Ferwerda was a man after God's heart. Everything about his actions toward me for the last several months had been completely honoring and genuine.

Well what do you know? After all my pleas to God over the week to give me yet another sign of the future of the relationship, I could see that God had been working in Steve's heart in a mighty way. There was no doubt that God was leading us together, I could not give up on our relationship. For the moment anyway, Steve seemed to know, too. He posted the letter in plain view in my office to remind us both of his promises to me.

Ahhh...we can all sit back and relax because the conflict is all resolved, right? It's time to get on with the happily ever after. Not so fast. You haven't seen anything yet...

Dive in the Deep
(Don't Fear the Unknown)

Obstacles are really opportunities for miracles in disguise. We don't appreciate anything in life that comes too easy, or that we don't have to learn to trust the Universe to work out. There's nothing more delightful than seeing impossible circumstances transform into beautiful stories.

Many boulder-sized, fear-inducing obstacles were brewing in Steve's and my relationship. I had only been back in town for a few days when I made a great discovery. *Absence* really does make the heart grow fonder, at least in our case. When I was out of town, Steve's heart couldn't stand to be without me. When I was in town, his mind started up a wrestling match again. Perhaps we were going to have to figure out how to be in a relationship in separate towns—the further away the better.

After another few weeks of his grueling confusion, I had a melt down. At our ages, and after eight months of a prayerful and patient relationship development with plenty of positive

Filling in the Middle

signs from every direction, I was pretty sure we'd had adequate time to make a wise, informed decision. Even Steve admitted he knew we were meant to be together. The question was no longer, "What is God telling you about the relationship?" Now the question was, "Steve, are you going to choose this best path for your life partner or not?"

God, I'm starting to feel anger and resentment toward Steve. He is so fickle, vacillating back and forth at the expense of my feelings. One day he wants me, the next he doesn't. I know there's a difficult battle going on inside him, but I'm having a hard time staying objective. The rejection really hurts every time. What do you want me to do?

My heart, as well as the hearts of my girls, was a growing risk factor. Steve is a natural with kids and had won over the affection and adoration of my girls long ago. Even they had begun asking questions about our future. "Are you going to marry mommy? We hope you are going to be our daddy."

Pulling away from the relationship, I began to construct a self-protective shell, something that hurt me to have to do. Maybe Steve should move somewhere else and decide what was important to him—a blond Barbie with no past, or a genuine brunette who loves God and is who she is today *because of* her past. I marveled as I noticed that my self-perception had healed immensely in this process.

Confused and frustrated, we sat down together with my insightful brother-in-law, asking him to help us discern our next move. Bruce gave us some very wise counsel, pointing out to us both that the goal of a healthy marriage wasn't about what we were getting for ourselves; it was about what we were giving to each other. He agreed that, indeed, it was time for us to make some decisions and suggested we take a week or two apart to devote ourselves to focused consideration on the matter. He seemed confident that this time of focused inquiry would clear things up about our future because God didn't want to play games with our hearts. The peace we felt after speaking to him confirmed many things we both felt already.

The Perfect Fit

Later that night, Steve loaded up his car for a ten-day trip. Some of his friends were building a house in a town a few hours away and had asked him to come and help. The timing was perfect. It was both exciting and frightening to know that we were about to make a decision that would determine the course of our future. Would we be together, or go our separate ways? I was quite ready for the closure of either option in order to get off the emotional roller coaster brought about by Steve's indecision. The ball was in his court. I could rest with either choice, knowing that I always had my first love by my side. Whatever happened, my future was God's, not Steve's. Still, I had to believe that God didn't lead me through the last several months for nothing.

A Big Upset

Remember the toothpaste incident and how I lied to protect myself from getting into trouble? Unfortunately, I learn my most impactful life lessons through undesirable choices or unwise decisions. And this time, the situation at hand was a tad bigger than toothpaste, which is probably why it was such a struggle for me to be honest.

Out of the blue the night he was getting ready to leave, Steve started questioning me about my past. This was totally uncharacteristic for him, but he kept digging, expressing that he had the nagging feeling that I was hiding something from him. The truth is, I *was* hiding something from him all this time, but it was something he knew literally nothing about and had no reason to doubt or question. I didn't even act guilty because I didn't think it would ever come up! The timing was uncanny, and he obviously wasn't giving in until I came clean. The only rational explanation that night was that God had put it on his heart to force me into the light.

Oh how I wished for the more simple days of toothpaste. When it comes to owning up to the skeletons in your closet that might come to light to harm your future, there are two options. Either open the door yourself, or you might get a little help at a

Filling in the Middle

most inopportune time. I have found that things are usually a lot less painful and messy when I take the initiative first.

Even though I had told Steve most of my past, I had failed to tell him about caving into temptation with Matt, the first Internet relationship after my divorce. First of all, I didn't think I could admit one more shameful thing to him, in light of his squeaky clean past. Secondly, when I admitted my past failures, I wanted him to perceive my life with some distance from the things I wasn't proud of. This one was so recent—so fresh—I couldn't bring myself to tell him about it. I tried to pretend it never happened, but apparently the Universe had other plans.

The ironic thing is that I did seek out advice from two of my spiritual advisors at the time and they both told me that I didn't need to bring up any more details of my past, that God had forgiven me so I didn't have to keep wallowing in regret. That is, all except for one. My good friend Sue was the single voice against the majority, confirming my greatest fear.

Sitting at her kitchen table, we sipped on her famous mocha's one morning when I admitted my dilemma. "Julie, you have to tell Steve the truth. Otherwise this guilt is going to plague you for your whole life. You won't ever be truly free because you'll worry that you'll be found out. Steve has to know everything, and you have to know he can accept it."

"But Sue, how can I? He'll never be able to handle this! It will be the death of the relationship for sure. I am scared...scared of the truth."

"You know what God is telling you to do. Don't you think you can trust Him with the outcome? Look what He has done so far. Your fear is unfounded. Remember what He said... "the truth will make you free" (John 8:32).

I suspected she was right about the need to be absolutely free from the fear of my past, but in the end, I ignored her advice. I wasn't about to get set up for more rejection, so I handled things in the way that seemed easiest. Instead of trusting God's intervention for the outcome, I caved in to fear. I so desperately wanted to put it all behind me that I accepted what I wanted to hear instead of what I needed to hear.

The Perfect Fit

What a costly decision this turned out to be. Here we were, hanging by a thread before Steve sped off into the sunset to decide the fate of our future, and I was still dragging him through the mud of my past.

When Steve looked into my eyes, searching for the answer to his question, I knew he could already see it. He waited for what seemed like an eternity for my honest answer, and I finally dragged it out like a mule with a grudge.

The pain and disappointment I saw reflected in his tear-filled eyes was heart wrenching. I had held out on him and opened myself up to appearing untrustworthy. If only I had told him sooner. If only I had listened and not allowed fear to control my life. The secret would have already been dealt with, but without the pain and distrust.

Okay God, I just splattered mud all over this window you brought into my life. I hope You've got enough Windex for this job. You promised me that the Son of grace and love would shine through to me with unfailing love. Here's Your chance to prove it. Somehow let the woman You have crushed rejoice.

Accounts Reviewable

Reinforcing my fears, Steve reacted about how I expected he would and my faith crumbled. I knew that he wouldn't be able to forgive me or to muster up the grace to put this in the past. Sending him off to think about a future together, I felt about as confident as a murder suspect caught on video.

I have heard it said that there are two kinds of pain in life—the pain of honesty and the pain of regret. How I wished on this day that I had succumbed to the pain of honesty, which weighs only ounces compared to the staggering weight of regret. It never occurred to me while I was indulging in the act of sensual impatience with someone whom I didn't love, that someday I'd have to be honest and accountable to another person for my actions. I didn't know that the careless behaviors of my past would someday deeply hurt someone in my future—someone besides me. I reasoned it was my life and my mistakes; I would

Filling in the Middle

be the only one to suffer from them. No one else would even have to know.

I don't believe that it's inflicting unnecessary self-torture to expect these drastic measures of honesty from oneself. On the contrary, it's done out of proactive liberation from allowing fear to control one's heart and mind, once again robbing happiness and wholeness. If Steve and I were to get married and we hadn't dealt with this issue, I would live out my marriage in bondage to shame and fear, always worried that Steve might somehow find out the truth. And anyhow, Steve deserved the truth about what he was getting himself into, including the possible risk of STDs. It was perhaps another "window" of opportunity for God's grace to shine through Steve, as so many times before, but at the moment felt more like a blackout blind.

The entire week we were apart, I had an urgent sense to pray for Steve. I figured there was plenty of ammunition in his already conflicted mind to drive the wedge between us even further, and my worry meter was off the charts. Would we be able to overcome this massive obstacle in our path?

The Power of Two

Remember Jackie, the beautiful-auburn haired woman who gave me hope that second chances for exciting, Divinely-inspired romance exists—even after divorce? I hadn't seen her since that first night several months earlier, but that very week we crossed paths again. Although I'd never cut her hair before, out of the blue she called and asked if I could work her into my schedule that week. Little did I know, this was more of a Divine appointment than a hair appointment.

Since Steve left, a dark cloud of despair and anxiety had followed me, constantly reminding me of all the seemingly insurmountable factors likely influencing him in contemplating our future. Recalling some of the story she had shared with me all those months ago, I wondered if some of her experiences would give me any hope. After several minutes of conversation, we moved into the subject of obstacles of our faith. Suddenly, I

The Perfect Fit

felt a compulsion to share my burden with her about the recent chain of events.

I told her about Steve not feeling strongly attracted to me and his confusion about spending his life with me, in spite of God giving us so many assurances and signs to pursue a future together. God had opened so many doors, it was absolutely clear to both of us that He wanted us together. When I told her the specifics she stared back in disbelief.

"Julie, when I met Joe, he wasn't attracted to me, either! He hated the color of my hair. I felt so rejected. Joe told me on several occasions that he thought I was a beautiful woman; I just wasn't physically what he envisioned his life mate would look like. But eventually he fell in love with my heart. He realized that in my heart, I was exactly the kind of wife he was looking for. This brought about a terrible conflict between his heart and his head. It was difficult to watch."

I listened intently. I could not believe the parallels of our stories, and the fact that she "just happened" to wander into my salon chair at this particular time. Her now husband fell in love with her mentally, emotionally and spiritually (ditto). He was moderately attracted to her, but not captivated (yup). He had not been married before and he was very hesitant to make a commitment (mmm hmmm), even though he knew God was telling him to take the plunge (can I get an amen!?).

"God even showed him very specifically one day in his prayer time that he was to marry me. God told Joe that He was about to go on into the 'Promised Land,' but he had to take the move of faith to get out of the desert." I imagined Joe, standing in the middle of the Sinai Desert, sweating and parched, staring down a Caribbean style oasis resort, complete with poolside palm trees and a tray of icy mojitos a few hundred meters up ahead, paralyzed with confusion about what to do.

If anyone could understand what I felt, watching the battle between head and heart, rivaling for the man I was supposed to share my future with, it was Jackie. This meeting was no coincidence.

Filling in the Middle

"Julie, I thought we would never get to that altar. Joe even had second thoughts after we picked out my wedding dress, a couple weeks before our wedding."

"So what did you do?"

"During the whole two-hour trip home in his car, I prayed for him," Jackie explained.

"Out loud?"

"Yes, I prayed fervently against the confusion he was experiencing until it passed."

"What was Joe doing while you prayed?" I couldn't imagine Joe welcoming prayer while he was struggling with confusion.

"He was driving...and listening. I didn't give him a choice. I knew God wanted me to pray. That's why I did it. And it was so worth it—we have a wonderful marriage. God got us through all that and He will get you through, too."

Jackie's sincerity and passion were contagious. She and Joe had been married for several years—several happy, exciting years. Joe even grew to love Jackie's hair.

I had no idea that Jackie had gone through almost exactly the same rejection and grief over her appearance. Several months earlier in our conversation, I heard only hope that such an inspiring romance existed. Now God randomly brought Jackie back into my life at just the right time for another purpose. Not only was she there to offer hope, I believed God sent Jackie to help me pray and so that I would feel less alone in my desperation. After hearing of her outcome, I knew that there was hope, against all odds, that God's divine plan for Steve and me would prevail. The burden I felt to pray over my situation was so heavy, it was almost paralyzing. God knew just what I needed when, and He provided.

On Tuesday of that week, Jackie and I got on our knees in her home for over an hour in heartfelt, focused, prayer for Steve's mind and heart. I don't think I've ever prayed so hard—or had the sense of absolute peace before leaving my knees—like I did that day. As we finished our prayer, Jackie confirmed that she too had the impression that our prayers had been heard and even answered.

The Perfect Fit

Disconnect From Feelings

The landscape inside my head got uglier than ever that week. Although I felt a shift in my heart during my prayer with Jackie, it seemed my mental health was constantly under attack with discouraging thoughts, extreme doubts, and depressed feelings.

Steve and I had agreed ahead of time not to talk on the phone much—if at all—and not to discuss our relationship with others, so that we could process God's leading in our hearts. He ended up calling me anyway about mid-week, and it sounded to me like he was having the time of his life, seeing old friends, and sort of...moving on. His aloof and carefree attitude made it seem like he didn't really miss me at all. In fact, he sounded happier than ever! It almost seemed like maybe he was giving me the hint that it was time for both of us to move on.

Meanwhile, back at the home front: *See how peaceful and happy he is now that you are out of the picture? He doesn't need you in his life. He's probably reconnecting with the girls he used to spend time around and doesn't have time to even think about you,* self-pity drawled in my ear. Oh, how I wished he hadn't called me, it only made me feel worse!

> "Sometimes faith is the absence of fear. Other times faith may be choosing to believe God even when your heart is melting with fear."[3] ~Beth Moore~

Dress by Faith

Even though Steve appeared to be stuck in the slow lane, it seemed like God continued moving me forward that week. With all the raging emotions going on inside of me, you wouldn't think I could deal with one more thing, but that's not usually how life rolls. It seemed we were on a tight schedule of some sort. To start with, since early spring when Steve and I talked about the increasing possibility of marriage, I had been unsuccessfully watching stores and magazines for a certain type of wedding dress "just in case."

That week—of all weeks—when things looked bleaker than ever, the sought after simple, white column dress was featured

Filling in the Middle

right on the cover of one of my new summer catalogs. Not only was the dress exactly what I had envisioned, it was on sale for thirty-five dollars! Steve had told me all along that if we got married, he wanted me to wear white because my slate was clean, and I would be his virgin bride.

God, I need help. I'm so confused. A future with Steve looks utterly impossible right now, and here I find the dress I've be looking for? Please forgive my doubt and my small faith but You know how discouraged I feel. Even though You assured me you've got this under control, I can't see it. Should I order it?

I never discerned an answer, but I realized this was the ideal time for me to show a little faith. It was time to stand firm—in spite of my miserable feelings and the odds—for what I believed God had told me. By faith, I would order the dress, doing my best to ignore my fears and feelings. Still, I was too embarrassed to tell anyone about ordering the dress.

Take a Dive

Inspirational music is one of the most spiritually healing medicines I know of, so when I heard from a friend that one of my favorite artists was giving a local concert that week, I needed to go. I craved a healing touch, and music had been that avenue so many times since my divorce.

During the concert, the musician stopped playing his guitar to share a story from his childhood. I was having a hard time focusing on the story at first. My unsettling thoughts started up their usual noisy chatter, until something in his story piqued my curiosity, drawing me in. It seemed to be a message prepared just for me.

When the artist was ten years old, his family moved to Hawaii. The apartment complex they moved into had a giant outdoor swimming pool and every day, he and his father and brother headed to the pool. The only problem was that, as a young boy, he was afraid of the water. He watched with longing as his Dad and older brother swam laps, performed tricks and dives, and made games of retrieving items from the bottom of the pool. One day he walked slowly over to his Dad by the deep

The Perfect Fit

end and asked, with grave apprehension, "Dad, will you teach me how to swim?"

"Son," his father said looking him in the eye, "if you want to learn to swim, you're going to have to jump in."

The boy thought his Dad was crazy. He couldn't imagine jumping in to the deep end of a swimming pool. He would drown! The two sat there by the pool for a long time, reasoning together. Dad consistently pointed to the deep end, indicating that his son must take the first step and jump in, the son fearful and hesitant to heed his Dad's instructions. Finally, after much coaxing and prodding, the son decided to trust. He mustered up the courage, closed his eyes, and jumped in. He came up sputtering and flailing and yelled, "Look Dad—I'm swimming!" Within a few days of practice, the boy was doing all the things his Dad and brother did, having the time of his life (Author's note: I don't recommend this method for teaching your children to swim).

One day his Dad came home from work and told the boys he was taking them down to the ocean to go snorkeling. They loaded up the car and drove a short distance to the local beach. When the boy took one look at that massive body of water with large breakers crashing into the shore, he felt sudden panic sweep over him. He wasn't too sure about this new level of adventure. I mean, the safety of the swimming pool was one thing, but the ocean? Finally, after coaxing from his Dad, he decided to take the risk to conquer his fears once again.

As he got into the water and started snorkeling, his fears melted away. The coral reef, the colorful fish, and the unusual aquatic life were so beautiful and so vibrant; it was one of the most incredible experiences he'd ever had. He realized that if he had given into his fears and stayed in the calm, protective water of the swimming pool, he would have missed the wonderful and incredible adventure that his father had arranged for him to experience.

Starting to play his guitar again softly, the musician explained that we need to trust God when He is moving us into something new, believing that it will be a beautiful adventure

Filling in the Middle

full of more blessings than we can imagine. But we must be willing to give up the security of what we know and where we feel safe in order to experience a new life.

Dropping clues about my future, God affirmed that this message was for me that night. Strangely, I had the sense that God was not only telling me that my imminent future was full of change, but I had a strong sense that night that He was telling me it would involve being uprooted from my comfortable and familiar surroundings. I almost laughed at the absurdity of the thought. In light of how things were going with Steve, not to mention the complicated circumstances of my life with divorce custody issues, I couldn't imagine being uprooted.

I am not qualified to analyze this message, God. I will wait for You to show me what You mean by all of this. I know you are preparing me for something, I just don't know what yet.

Whatever it was to be, I heard the deeper message loud and clear. It was time to jump into unknown waters so I could experience the splendor and magnitude of the deep.

The Perfect Fit

Step 4: Placing the Last Piece

When you get down to the last few pieces of your puzzle, something akin to frenzy takes over. There's a focused mission to finish.

Even though God wasn't influenced by my frenzied feelings, I anxiously looked over His shoulder, impatient to see things resolved. But as He reached for those last few pieces, I stared wide-eyed in anticipation. There was nothing quite so treasured as His placing that last piece. Where a few minutes ago I couldn't wait to be done, suddenly I hesitated; savoring the moment for which I had waited so long.

All those difficult moments, complex details, and labor-intensive experiences added up to the beautiful and complete picture that, only moments before, was entirely obscure.

The Perfect Fit

Lemons before Lemonade
(Contrasts Are Sweeter)

When Steve returned from his trip ten days later on Saturday, June 19, 1999, we made arrangements to take my daughters on a picnic before he headed out again to Denver to close the sale of his puzzle company. Upon arriving at the desired picnic location, fifty miles from home, we spent the morning hiking around several acres of interesting sandstone formations and early Native American petroglyphs. The bright, sunny day belied the cloud of anxiety that still hovered over me from the previous ten days.

From the moment he pulled into my driveway that morning, Steve's unusually aloof manner was not what you would expect from a man getting together with the girl he wanted to marry. I couldn't tell from his poker face if he was holding a "full house" in his future or on the verge of folding, but I could tell you that if something didn't give soon, there was going to be a royal flush!

For the sake of the girls, we kept the conversation on a nice surface level over lunch. I was both eager and scared to hear what God had been saying to him regarding our relationship, but now the awkwardness between us felt reminiscent of a first date. I tried to keep my expectations low after the disheartening goodbye and the few short, matter-of-fact conversations we'd had while he was away, but nothing had prepared me for the grief and anger I now felt in reaction to his flippant and cool manner toward me. Instinctively I knew even before he said it, what he was going to say.

Doesn't he look chipper over there eating his turkey sandwich, now that he's off the hook? He's probably excited to get back to Denver so he can find Patty Pure. Excuse me if I sound a wee bit snippy, God. But after all we've been through, now what? I can't believe that I have invested all this time, energy, and prayer into this relationship and this is what I get? Why did you lead me into this, knowing he wouldn't be able to

The Perfect Fit

follow through? I trusted You not to let me get hurt and let me down! I laid my will down so many times but You just kept encouraging me in this direction. What about the assurance You gave me after prayer with Jackie—where is the victory now? I don't know who I'm angrier at—You or that sorry creation of Yours over there.

I was thankful that God was big enough to handle my honest feelings, because I sure was having trouble with them. My angry and despairing prayers were constant throughout the day. How could God let me down like this? I was so anxious to retreat to my home and be done with it all—be done with him. Mechanically, I started packing up the lunch while the girls were off capturing unsuspecting "horny toads" in the sagebrush (hey, that's what we call them in Wyoming).

Coming over to help me pack up the leftovers, Steve finally spoke up.

"Julie, I know you are probably wondering what I'm thinking about us...after our time apart and all."

"Sure...you are probably wondering the same about me."

"Why don't you go ahead and start."

"You brought it up, you go first." I sure wasn't going to show my cards until he did. Maybe there was still hope. Maybe he'd been holding back because of my obvious distant attitude today (hiding my feelings is not a strong point). Maybe...

"I'm glad we had this time apart. I've really had some great times of prayer and reflection. But...well...I guess I don't feel quite ready to make a decision yet. I'm still not sure how I feel about our relationship. Since I'm going to Denver today, I thought we could take another week...give it just a little more time. When I get back from this trip, I will for sure have a decision for you."

That's it? You still don't know how you feel about me? Well Steve, I guess you're the only person whose life and feelings matter in this situation. It seems you are the only one who has a decision to make. I guess I'll appear to grovel a bit longer until you are ready to give me your verdict.

Placing the Last Piece

Through hot tears, I crammed everything in the picnic basket and started toward the car, not trusting myself to speak. How dare he be so arrogant and careless with my feelings—as if I was just hanging around waiting for him to decide if he loved me or not! In that moment, I felt somewhat worthless.

I once thought that the people over at Harlequin Romance Company made up all that ridiculous material. I used to wonder who would buy that unrealistic stuff. Now I was living it.

Digging his lame hole deeper he threw in for effect, "I just don't know if I will make a good dad...I'm not sure if I'm that good with kids."

Argh! If I had been one millimeter less mature at that moment, I would have kicked him in the shins. The utter stupidity of his statement was almost more than I could take. After spending the whole day running around, teasing, and playing with the girls, he earned their adoring and trusting looks just as he had done so easily for the last six months. He was a natural with kids! He had a special connection with my daughters and I couldn't believe he was so dense he didn't see what great dad material he was.

Not only did my kids love his tender and playful nature, other kids he didn't even know gravitated to him—at church, at the park, practically everywhere we went, largely because he was a kid at heart himself. Either he didn't see himself like others did or he was looking for any excuse to get out while he still could.

With all he put me through that day, intense feelings of resentment and dislike welled up until I thought I would burst like a water balloon. But I couldn't let him see me cry. No, my pride wasn't about to let him know what was going on inside of me, even though I was having a little trouble concealing my hurt, anger, and disappointment. Like when I *accidentally* spilled my cup of red Kool-Aid all over his white shirt...or when I *accidentally* pushed him into that den of rattle snakes...or when I *accidentally* left him out in the boonies and made him hitchhike fifty miles back to town. Hey, a gal can have her fantasies, can't she?

The Perfect Fit

Groundhog Day Replay

We decided to hang out with the girls and their newfound horny toads for a few minutes before heading back to town. I continued to act indifferent and cold toward Steve, longing for this to all be behind me. But deep inside, I couldn't ignore my intense feelings of disappointment. It would take a long while for my bruised heart to move on.

I thought about all the things I loved about Steve—the happy heart, the smile that lit up his whole face, the playful, romantic streak, and how he constantly did things to serve me and show me how much he cared. He lived his faith, told the truth, and was his own, secure person. He loved hugs, reading books with me, and engaging in sports together. He was my best friend, and I felt more comfortable with him than any man I'd ever met. We already shared so many warm, happy memories together, and once again the loss of dreams seemed more than I could bear.

Where was the promised victory? How could my fragile, budding faith endure this setback and ever again interpret God's leading with confidence? Did Steve miss the signs or did I? No. I couldn't let myself start down that path of thinking again. Reflecting back on all that had happened; I had not heard God wrong. Perhaps I misunderstood how He was going to use the situation in my life, but I knew I had not heard Him wrong. It was on that day that I realized Steve was going to miss out on a part of God's beautiful plan for his life.

I knew if Steve hadn't been able to determine over the previous ten days that he wanted to spend the rest of his life with me, another week wasn't going to make a difference. The relationship was over—at least for now. Already he was putting out feelers for jobs out of the area. He'd had two interviews the previous week—including one out of state. Our relationship wouldn't be strong enough to survive being apart again, because I had given up hope. I wasn't going to keep setting myself up for more pain, going back and forth like a ball in a ping-pong match. No, there was nothing he could determine in a few more days that he didn't already know. If God were going

Placing the Last Piece

to change Steve's heart on the matter, He would have to do it somewhere else.

On the forty-five minute drive back to Riverton, Steve and I didn't say one word to each other. I'm sure it was apparent to all that I was "in a mood." We'd taken my car and I was driving, so I put a compilation CD in the player and began singing along, a great way to avoid talking. Suddenly an old Amy Grant song started playing, and I realized how fitting the words were as soon as they left my mouth. To make a point, I turned the volume way up, belting out a duet with Amy, "Lead me on, lead me on..." When the song came to the end, I hit replay. I know how childish it sounds, but I couldn't seem to stop myself.

Halfway through the ride home—and the fifth time through the song—I sneaked a glance at him. He looked like Odie (Garfield's dog) sitting over in the passenger seat, practically panting with a happy-go-lucky, nonchalant expression on his face, he was oblivious to his song dedication. I wanted to wipe that infuriating happy-dog look off his face. How could he stomp all over my heart like this and be so unaffected? Maybe he wasn't as tenderhearted and compassionate as I thought. Finally, a sweet little voice came from the back seat.

"Mommy, could we please change the song now?"

When we got back to my house, I was more than happy to drop him off so he could get his car and leave town for Denver. I needed to be alone to work through my feelings. One of my favorite things to do when I am intensely angry is to go out into my back yard, get the log splitter, and split wood. There's just something really satisfying about swinging a big axe around, destroying things. Unfortunately, when I got to my back yard, I noticed my woodpile was already reduced to a pile of kindling sticks from many other therapy sessions, so I was going to have to find another outlet. But first I had to drop the girls off at their dad's and then take a few hair appointments I'd scheduled at the salon. All I wanted to do was be alone to cry. I could surely sympathize with Chippy, the canary! The song in my heart was long gone.

The Perfect Fit

In the middle of my first late-afternoon appointment, Steve stopped by the salon to tell me goodbye. I knew I hadn't been very nice to him without even so much as a "goodbye" for a sendoff.

I *couldn't* say goodbye.

He must finally be feeling bad about being so careless with my feelings, I thought when I saw the bouquet of flowers he brought with him.

The words he said next, however, only made me upset all over again. "I will miss you while I'm in Denver. I love you, Julie."

How dare he say such confusing words at a time like this! One thing I hate is being pacified. You know, when someone is trying to appease your anger...especially when they are the source of it! I knew this was what he was doing. He was telling me what I wanted to hear so that he could assuage his guilt. I coolly accepted the flowers—Amy Grant's song still playing in my head—and I half-heartedly gave him a hug, wishing with all my heart that he really meant it. I appreciated his feeble effort to assuage my feelings of rejection, but it wasn't going to erase the hurt.

Earlier, I'd made plans to go to the movie with my Mom after I finished my afternoon appointments. The kids were staying with their dad for the night, and normally I would have been looking forward to an evening with Mom. But when the time came, I was too distracted and restless. After barely surviving the intense week, and now this even worse day, I explained to my Mom that I was going home to lick my wounds in privacy.

The Scavenger Hunt

When I arrived at my house, I almost stepped on the card lying on the floor just inside the front door. The card had pansies arranged on top of it—one of my favorite flowers. Inside the envelope was a letter telling me that he'd planned a little scavenger hunt for me. *Oh great!* This was a super time to play games with me—just what I needed after a day like today. I mean, was this guy so insensitive that he could stomp all over

Placing the Last Piece

my heart and then make me feel better with a game? I had to admit that it must have taken some time and effort to plan. At least he was starting to think of me, even if it was a little too late.

Something was taped to the bottom of the card. A *piece of a puzzle?* According to the instructions, I was to find a puzzle piece and word with each clue in the hunt, and then put them together in sequence. After assembling them, I would discover a secret message.

I might as well play along, and then I can drown my sorrows over a bag of cookies.

The scavenger hunt had thirty clues, so it kept me busy for a while. True to the directions, each clue had a piece of puzzle and a word attached. Since I had all night to put words and puzzle pieces together, and since I was getting rather focused on finding the next clue, I didn't follow his exact instructions to put them together in sequence as I found them.

The twenty-eighth clue instructed me to go to the mailbox for the second to last clue, where another card and puzzle piece were waiting. The mailbox was a block away, so I walked quickly to retrieve the "mail." The card, sitting in my mailbox, had all of the words put together for me. I could hardly breathe as I read the words on the page.

"There is hope for your future," says the LORD, "for I have given rest to the weary and joy to the sorrowing." Jeremiah 31: 17, 25 (NLT)

The Jigsaw Jig
(The Proposal)

"Dear Julie, God has blessed me richly in my first thirty-three years and made my life a beautiful jigsaw puzzle. It's missing a piece though, and that piece is…_____. For the last piece, go to the dining room table."

The Perfect Fit

This can't be...was he...is this...? My mind swirled with the possibilities. Maybe he really was "leading me on" all day—in a way I didn't suspect—to throw me off the trail of his true intentions. Maybe I should have followed his directions and put the puzzle together as I went. Oops.

Stepping back into my house, *there was music playing in the background!* The beautiful love song by Stephen Curtis Chapman greeted me from the stereo with, "I Will Be Here." Steve sat at my dining room table, holding a piece of puzzle and two long stemmed fire and ice roses (red roses tipped with white edges). I will never forget the intense, joyous look of love I saw in his misty eyes. It was the most breath-taking moment of my life, especially with the contrasting backdrop of the day behind it, the anxious week on my knees, and the deep love in my heart for this man. Even though it was all supposed to happen this way, it took me by surprise. *God took me by surprise.*

I sat down at the table, cheeks wet with tears, to put all the pieces of the puzzle together to reveal a photograph of Steve and me taken months earlier. On a picture perfect street in Breckenridge, Colorado, during our first ski trip the previous New Year's Eve, we stood by a beautifully decorated Christmas tree, weighed down by large glass bulbs and snow-covered branches. With our arms draped around each other, rosy-cheeked smiles reflected happy hearts. A thousand words of love emanated from our faces before we were even aware of it—a love put there by the One who made us for each other.

When I got down to the last missing piece that Steve held in his hand—my face—he handed it over for me to symbolically put in place as the finishing touch. The picture was now complete. Getting down on one knee and grasping my hands in his, Steve said tenderly, through laughter and tears, "Dear Julie, God has blessed me richly in my first thirty-three years and made my life a beautiful jigsaw puzzle. It's missing a piece though...and that piece is...*you.* I love you. Will you marry me?"

A huge grin spreading across my face, I laughed—and cried—my answer. "Yes!"

Placing the Last Piece

Taking me into his arms, we laughed and cried and hugged some more. You could have scooped up the joy in the room with a snow shovel.

After several minutes of reveling in our joy, he placed the two fire and ice roses in my hand. "Julie, these symbolize our love. The red on the base of the rose represents my love for you. The white on the tips represents your purity to me. While I was in Jackson, I picked out something else for you—for us."

Pulling out a beautiful silver band, he placed the engagement ring on my finger. He'd picked it out the previous week while we were apart, the dork! He even purchased an engagement ring for himself—a Turkish puzzle ring—to remind him that I am the missing piece to his puzzle.

What a bozo I'd been. These last few days I had made things much more difficult for myself than they needed to be, with too many assumptions and pity parties, and too little faith. If I had any maturity level at all, I wouldn't have acted so impetuously. This whole week, I'd mistaken his happy, carefree attitude for cold-hearted aloofness, and I couldn't have been more wrong. He'd been planning to ask me to marry him for several days, but he had to act aloof that day so as not to give away the surprise.

The steady stream of laughter flowed as we talked about the day leading up to this moment. In all my life I had never experienced so many different, intense emotions in one day.

"I think I owe you an apology." I sheepishly grinned at him.

"What for?"

"For acting like a crabby two-year-old all day. I am so sorry. I had no idea why you were acting the way you were. I was so feeling sorry for myself."

"I understand. I really tried to throw you off because I know how hard you are to surprise and I wanted so badly to surprise you."

"I'm surprised, all right! Where were you hiding while I was on the big scavenger hunt?"

"In the bathtub."

The Perfect Fit

"One of the clues was in the bathroom. That was pretty risky! Just out of curiosity, when did you decide to ask me to marry you?"

"I've known since Tuesday." *Tuesday!* That was the day Jackie and I had been on our knees together—the day I felt God whisper that the spiritual battle was won! How exciting! God wasn't misleading me after all. I was just too caught up looking at my circumstances—the crashing ocean waves below my feet—instead of trusting.

"Man do I ever have a lot to tell you!" I snickered.

Thinking over how it all had played out, I had no regrets. True, I'd just spent one of the most difficult weeks in a long time. But I noticed that, compared to all the anxiety I'd suffered during the week, the beauty and joy of this moment was spectacular! I could finally relax as I basked in the comfort of his love and commitment to me, based on our previously discussed convictions about the implications of "engagement." We decided together that if we were to ever become engaged, the commitment would be as serious as wedding vows. Engagement would no longer be a "trial period," but only the time we would need to plan the wedding. My heart was so light it felt like it would just float right out of my chest. Steve Ferwerda had just committed his life and future to me.

Telling Secrets

Although I'm a pretty good secret-keeper, I just love when the time comes to tell them. There were so many things that God had showed me over the course of our relationship—things I didn't dare tell Steve until now, because I didn't want to put pressure on him or get ahead of God. I knew God would reveal what Steve needed to know at the proper times.

But now, as Steve and I discussed the plans of our immediate future, I grabbed the cream pitcher in my kitchen containing the ever-present reminder of God's promise to me. With a mischievous grin I set it down in front of him.

"Steve, sitting in this little dish is the biggest and best secret that I have ever kept from anyone."

Placing the Last Piece

"What is it?" Knitting his brows with curiosity, he pulled out a dry, shriveled up white rose.

I explained to him about the wedding and the whole white rose incident, how God promised me a very special man in my future, and how I had asked God to give me white roses from my future husband as a special sign.

"When did I give you white roses?"

"Remember the petals on the bottom of the Valentine's bag you sent home with me on the plane?"

"Oh, that's why you asked me later that night why I gave you white roses!" The lights were coming on.

"Yes! See how significant that night was to me? And that was way back in January! But there's more. Remember the night you told me about the 'Purity Test' you took at work? When you told me that night you were still a thirty-two-year-old virgin, the realization hit me that a white rose symbolizes purity. That talk back in December was a powerful first indication to me that you were the one. I believed I would receive a white rose *from the man*, but I didn't know that the white rose would *be the man*! Then when you gave me the white rose petals, I knew it for sure!" You are my white rose.

"That's amazing! I can't believe you could keep all this to yourself for so long. I'm speechless with all that God was up to behind the scenes! He has done so much for us!"

> Now to him who is able to do immeasurably more than all we ask or imagine, according to his power that is at work within us. Ephesians 3:20

Standing up from the table, I grabbed his hand. "We have to go over to share our news with Mom and Dad! They'll be so surprised!"

"Not exactly." Steve gave me a sly wink.

"What do you mean?"

"I called your Dad on Wednesday to get his permission first."

"No way! He knew I was having a hard week and he didn't let on at all. I didn't realize you would ask his permission."

The Perfect Fit

"Are you kidding? Not ask a guy with biceps as big as basketballs? I wouldn't do it any other way!" Even at fifty-nine, my Dad could double as Popeye.

"Hey, I want to go over to see them, but not quite yet. I have a few secrets I want to tell you about, too."

"Really?"

"Remember the night I drove to Rawlins, after spending Christmas with you?"

"You mean the night you were cutting up onions in the car?"

"Yeah—that's the one. Well, what I never told you is that, God told me in the car that night, "This is the girl—she's the one I've saved you for all these years."

"So...would you say your tears were because you were stuck with me, or because you still had to go through Rawlins?"

"Definitely Rawlins! Actually, I was so emotional because I knew God was telling me that the wait was finally over, and that you were going to be my wife. The tears were like a sign from Him because I've never cried like that in my life. I couldn't control them, but they were also accompanied by incredible joy. I've also realized over the last week that God was partly responsible for holding back my feelings for you until the time was right because we had some necessary steps to take that couldn't be rushed or cut short. But I'm so sorry about the times I've hurt you."

"So how did you resolve the attraction problem?"

"Let's get this straight. I think you are really beautiful. In fact, the more I get to know you, the more beautiful you become to me. It's never been that I'm not attracted to you or that I don't think you are pretty. It was more that I had certain ideals—some of which I had no right to put my hope in. I don't know when they all started, but I know that marrying a woman should be most about her inner beauty and virtue. When we've been married fifty years, I doubt we're going to love each other for how we look. We can't put any hope in that. I realized how prideful I was. I hope you can forgive me. I think you're really beautiful. Even more than that, I love your heart. I love what

Placing the Last Piece

God has done in your life and I can't wait to spend my life with you."

The week we were apart Steve read the book, *Should I Get Married,* by M. Blaine Smith, designed to help Christian singles work through confusing issues while deciding to get married or not. One thing he read is that an excellent marriage candidate does not necessarily meet our idealistic expectations. Even so, there should be moderate physical attraction between two people who are contemplating marriage. The bigger questions to ask are about the lasting things. *What are this person's values, goals, expectations, and personality? What does this person's spirit look like? Do they have a passion for God?* Those are the things that matter. That is basically what Steve and I had done before we got engaged—asked all the hard questions possible and contemplated the lasting things. We also discussed our expectations of marriage and of each other using in-depth pre-marriage discussion guide we found online, *Talk it Out Before You Say I Do.*

Knowing that Steve really loved me for my heart, my values, and my growing character—not for my appearance—brought unexpected joy and security. Eventually, I was able to accept my humble position beside the "international ski model."

It takes a Village

Sitting in my parent's living room, we excitedly discussed wedding plans. Steve's sister and father were already planning a visit from the Middle East. Could we possibly put a wedding together in five short weeks? We agreed that night that we should indeed plan to be married when his family could be a part of this most special event of our lives. There would be so much to plan, but none of which seemed daunting or burdensome. In fact, I looked forward to planning this day with great anticipation.

After firming up our initial plans over iced tea, we told my family all that we'd seen God do to bring us together. I had spared them many details while waiting upon God to work things out, keeping quiet about all the treasured secrets He had

The Perfect Fit

shown me. Because of my usual habit of analyzing and discussing all the details of my life with them, they were amazed by all the secrets I now disclosed for the first time.

And then there were the people God used in our lives! God is so *previous*; it's mind-boggling! He goes before you, weaving people and circumstances ahead of time into the fabric of your picture, before you are aware of it.

Such was the case with the girl that had been giving us airline tickets. From Christmas until the end of March, Steve and I were able to see each other every two or three weeks, primarily because of the free tickets. At the end of March, when he was ready to move to Riverton, the girl from the airport called to tell me that she could no longer offer me the buddy passes. She explained that the airline employees had new restrictions on the quantity of tickets they were entitled to, and she needed them for her relatives. God's purpose for those tickets was completely fulfilled just before she called.

Pastor Charlie had been the one to remind me that God's best would find me "even if God had to bring him in from the next state or across the world." How funny that Steve was both of those. Charlie had given hours of wise, solid counseling to help me wait for God's best for me, and then he helped us get the right start in our lives together.

Then there was Jackie. She played a vital role previous to the relationship by introducing me to the possibilities of an exciting God-initiated, inspiring romance. After her first appearance, she entered the stage once again to play her part for the grand finale, by helping me win a crucial battle on our knees. Jackie's role in my life indeed brought hope.

Terry and Sandi, the couple that Steve lived with in Colorado when we met, provided encouragement and insight for Steve in addressing his fears about stepping into a blended family. They were both previously divorced and had raised a blended family together. Fortunately, their experiences were mostly positive, and they were able to put to rest most of Steve's fears and concerns about marrying someone in my situation.

Placing the Last Piece

My brother-in-law, Bruce, had given us wise advice on numerous occasions for a healthy spiritual perspective. He was very instrumental in helping clear up the hesitation and confusion, especially at the end.

My sweet daughters were so accepting and loving toward Steve. From day one they made him feel special and wanted, unlike so many kids who feel threatened by a "new dad" figure in their lives. To prove their love, they forced him to accompany them to Dairy Queen on several occasions. Steve in turn had also accepted them and shown them tangible love by spending lots of time with them playing sports, helping with schoolwork, wrestling on the floor, reading to them, and praying with them. On one occasion, he even donned a "Mrs. Doubtfire" persona when he came to watch them for the day while I worked. They were so shocked when they saw him that they started giggling and jumping on him.

We can't forget my own parents. Their role may have been the most important of all. Not only did they provide the bride, they kept the freezer stocked with ice cream during the budding romance. According to Steve, that sealed the deal as far as he was concerned!

The Second Proposal

A few days later when they returned from their dad's house, Steve got down on bended knee before my unsuspecting daughters, delicate pink roses in hand, and took their small hands in his. He tenderly read a letter he had written to them to express his future love and devotion as their step-dad. As he read, each face wore their own expressive emotions—wide eyes and grins of delight on the girls' faces, and tears of tender love moistening his.

"I have grown to love you both very much. ...God has given your mom and myself a very special love for each other, and we have decided that we want to spend the rest of our lives together. I'd like to ask you to be my daughters. I promise to love you always and to always try to be the best possible father to both of you. I promise to always love your mom and that I will never, ever, ever leave her. I want to be there as you continue to grow into beautiful young women. I love you." Handing them the roses, he impatiently asked, "Well, what do you say?"

"Yes!" They both screamed at the same time while jumping up and down. "When?"

"Soon. We are working on that." After giant hugs they continued dancing around the living room, squealing with glee.

What dreams were re-established for all of us that day! Now my girls would have a dad in my home that loved them as his own. This love was a precious gift, coming from a man who was not their biological father. Steve was their window of God's love, too. There was still time left for them to experience a real family life in my home, something they had missed out on pretty much since birth. God had been so good to give them this gift while they were young enough to accept it willingly and joyfully.

The Forgotten Purchase

Hanging up newly washed clothes in the girls' closets later that day, I noticed the two white gauze dresses with delicate hand-made appliqué pansies waiting forgotten in the recesses.

You thought of everything, God. You've been putting this wedding together for over a month! Thank You so much.

While shopping with my mom in a clothing boutique in our hotel in Mexico in May, I came across these two precious little girl dresses. They were unlike any I had ever seen, with the colorful handcrafted silk pansies giving them a look of sweet innocence against the sturdy white gauze. I kept coming back to them in the boutique, unable to forget about them. Even though they were above my budget, I felt a desire to splurge. When I got them home, the girls loved them as much as I did, although I explained that we would have to save them for a special occasion. That time was now—the dresses were perfect for a wedding.

Placing the Last Piece

To the Last Detail

When God arranges something in our lives in His time and His way, He doesn't leave out any pieces. The puzzle He puts together is a complete, stunning picture. Now that Steve and I would be getting married, he needed a stable job with a good income to help support his new family. One of his reservations about asking me to marry him was his desire to have a job in place first. Even after spending much time looking for work in our town, jobs for his qualifications were scarce.

The day before Steve proposed, he got a job offer in a wintry ski town in northwest Wyoming. The timing couldn't have been more perfect, giving Steve the assurance and confidence in God's provision for the future.

When Steve told me about his job offer and asked me what I thought about moving, I sat in silent contemplation. For the first time in years, I was finally safe and comfortable in my little spot in the world. I'd had enough change in the last five years of my life to rival a Wyoming weather report. A few weeks ago I would have begged him to stay in Riverton and look for work, holding onto my safety zone with white knuckles. But something had changed.

God had been preparing me just for this moment—to let go of fear and be willing to "dive in" to the unknown. The night of the music concert, God indeed began preparing me for a move. He wanted me ready and willing to embark on a more exciting reef adventure away from my safe little swimming pool, even if it did feel like we were moving to the North Pole.

Sure, I would prefer something a little more tropical. But things could be worse—Steve could have gotten a job in Rawlins! No matter what, holding on to my safe, comfortable life and routine would not be worth missing all that He had arranged for me to experience. For this huge life change, He knew I needed time to adjust to the thought ahead of time, before the moment of decision. Because of God's loving preparation, I could answer Steve's inquisitive and hopeful eyes with my own twinkle. "Do you think we could bring the hot tub?

Dream about the Day
(July 23, 1999)

With only five weeks to prepare for a wedding, our lives were a flurry of activity! We felt God's providing hand, helping us work out every last detail in a relatively easy and quick manner. Things went into place so easily; the planning was practically effortless.

The dress I ordered the week Steve was gone came in and fit perfectly. My parents agreed to host the wedding at their beautiful country home with spectacular views of the local mountains. All of Steve's immediate family and a few other relatives were able to make last minute arrangements to be here from places like Lebanon, Egypt, New Hampshire, Denver, Michigan, California, and Colorado. A local nursery loaned us—for free—several large flowering pots to adorn the lawn. My mom and her friends offered to decorate and to cater all the food for the reception. Pastor Charlie, who had counseled us during our relationship, was available that weekend to perform our wedding ceremony. We found a professional photographer in the middle of wedding season with only five weeks notice—who did an excellent job and charged us a fraction of what the other professional photographers in the area charge. Our entire wedding only cost about four hundred dollars, because we had so many people contributing. That kind of savings helped provide for one other important occasion—the honeymoon.

Ah yes, the honeymoon. One of our favorite discount travel websites had last minute mega-specials to Cozumel, Mexico, the perfect place for quiet honeymoon bliss. The last minute deal on the charter trip was even scheduled to leave the day after our wedding from Denver. Every little detail of our wedding miraculously fell into place.

Just think about it. If I had gone my own way all those times instead of allowing God to realign me to His best path, not trusting Him or His plan for good in my life, but instead had resorted to my old patterns in order to try to make myself happy, I would have missed all of this! Sure, I might have been cruising down a road somewhere in a red convertible, but as a miserable and lonely person. This was true happiness. This was a supernatural adventure. *This was worth waiting for!*

Mid-Summer Night's Dream

Friday, July twenty-third, dawned bright and sunny. The evening wedding, planned outdoors at my parent's home, was a dream come true. Since I was a young girl, I had always dreamed of having my wedding at, what was then, my grandparent's home. Situated on thirteen acres overlooking the beautiful Wind River Mountain Range, the historic two-story white house was the perfect setting. Everything about this childhood playground of mine was full of carefree happy memories. The large rolling green lawn had hosted many a summer hide-and-seek game, the scenic pond teemed with bull frogs, hoping not to be caught for the hundredth time, fruit trees ripened for tasty pies, billowing flower beds provided splashes of color, and the ivy-covered walls and fences were all a part of what I loved about this familiar place. I couldn't think of a more fitting location for one of the happiest days of my life.

The evening of the wedding was a typical, mid-summer evening with flowers in bloom, the smell of freshly cut grass, and the lowering sun kissing a golden glow upon everything it touched. While the guests arrived and were seated in chairs on the lawn, we played our pre-recorded favorite music to set the mood. The whole picture was enough to make a person shed sentimental tears, even without a wedding.

Whenever God shows up somewhere, He just can't seem to come without bringing His two companions along, peace and joy. God's presence blanketed our wedding ceremony with a surreal beauty and peace that was as tangible as the visible golden rays of the sun, bathing everything in its path. Our friends and family could sense it, commenting that they couldn't quite articulate how very special this event felt to them. Even my Dad—not the touchy-feely sentimental type—

whispered into my ear after the ceremony, "This is the most beautiful wedding I have ever experienced."

We planned the event to be symbolic and meaningful, rather than traditional. We wanted it to be a personal testimony to our guests of all God had done in our lives, and how He wanted to touch their lives with His redeeming power as well. After reading our vows to each other, Steve got down on his knees and called my daughters over to him. He read them their very own set of vows, promising to love them and to love me the very best he could for his whole life.

Much to his surprise, as soon as he had finished his vows to them, the girls broke into an acapella song by Nat King Cole, "Love Was Made for Me and You." When these two tender exchanges had taken place—his vows and their pure-pitched heartfelt song—there wasn't a dry eye in the yard. In fact, there were so many tears shed that night, that my Dad didn't have to use the sprinklers for a couple of days.

A New Beginning

After the last of the guests had finally left, we said goodbyes to our families. We were so grateful for all they had done to make our wedding day smooth and magical. Steve's family would all be returning home to the far corners of the world, which is why we had chosen to spend the whole day together with them, instead of following tradition. My parents had worked like beavers to get their house and yard ready for all the guests, setting up all the chairs and tables, and getting the food and decorations ready for the reception.

Driving away from my parent's home late that evening, we reminisced together about the wonderful day behind us, and planned for the wonderful future ahead of us.

"Julie?"

"Yes?" I snuggled close to my new husband.

"Thanks for marrying me."

"Thanks for asking." I said dreamily, laying my head on his shoulder.

"You looked so beautiful today. Wow. I can't believe we're actually married."

"I know what you mean. Do you feel any different?" I asked, as the lights of Rawlins came into view.

"Not yet." He winked at me. "I can't wait to start our lives together."

"We already have. And we get to start it right now...in Rawlins. How ironic."

Maneuvering the car against the usual gale force winds while driving into town, we giggled at all the tumbleweed blowing across the highway.

"Hey," Steve nudged me as we pulled up the first convenience store on our way into town.

"Yeah?"

"Uh...can I get some ice cream?"

"Sure—as long as you get me one of those cookie ice-cream sandwiches."

Some things never change.

The True Romance

Living in this world, it's so hard to imagine even one event where there is no disappointment. Our wedding was just such a day. It was the most beautiful and memorable day of my life, better than any fairytale I'd ever read. It was the closest possibility I have on this earth to spending a day with my Creator.

I'd like to think that when we are living our lives in awareness that there is a larger purpose and meaning for us, that we are able to experience at least one moment that can never be forgotten—a moment that is satisfying and beautiful and maybe even...*perfect*. Time seems to stand still for that precious instant, giving us a glimpse and a hope of what's possible in a better than average life.

The day I became Steve's wife was one of those magical moments. Oh how I wished I could hold on to that feeling for more than just a day. I don't think in all my life I ever imagined a moment as sweet and pure and lovely.

The Designer of love and romance holds out the offering for all of us to experience a very special story full of inspiring details and a future of hope. We don't have any guarantees what is in store for us, but a life connected to our Source life *is the romance.* So take a risk. Give God the pieces of your life and see how He can arrange them into a beautiful picture—into a whole gallery of artistic splendor. He has a new puzzle waiting just for you, one that will lavish you with His unfailing love, goodness, and faithfulness.

Earthly marriage should not be our goal. Falling in love with God, the creator of all good stories, now that's something worth living for.

Today is the first day of the rest of your eternity. Your Knight in shining armor is waiting. Spend it falling in love like never before.

Epilogue
Restored Dreams

Sitting down at the table to read my Bible one morning in the spring of 2000, I pulled out a piece of onion-skin paper. Carefully opening it, I read the shaky handwriting that brought the familiar words before me once more. "I see that God is giving you the desires of your heart, just like He did for me." Those were the words that Steve's mom wrote in her final letter to me over a year ago. Pondering them, I suddenly realized for the first time what she meant. It was a secret message meant just for me. *She knew I was the one—the woman she had prayed about for over thirty years to stand by her son through this life.*

When Marian Ferwerda was a young missionary wife and mother, her husband was killed in an airplane crash. She was left a widow with two small boys (Steve's older brothers), and a set of her own broken dreams for full-time life missionary work in the Middle East. Eventually she reconnected with an old family friend from the mission field, John Ferwerda. When he asked her to marry him, not only did he restore her dreams for the mission field, but also he provided her sons with a loving father, reviving her dreams for an intact, loving family.

Her comment had significant meaning for me. It was her way of reaching out in grace to identify a common thread in our lives of being thrust into the world husbandless, our children fatherless in our own homes, and our dreams broken. In spite of the differences in how our commonality emerged, she used it as a bridge to me, not a barrier. She believed my future was to be blessed with a union to her son, the same way that John Ferwerda blessed her life in so many ways, restoring her dreams. God had answered her prayer for her son and she got to see it before she died.

It would only make sense that God, in His goodness, let this woman of strong faith be assured of His provision. For in her Bible she kept a written prayer, discovered after her death, imploring for God not to "take her home" until her last unmarried son found a wife. She felt that, until he had a wife by his side, he needed her to be in his life to encourage him, and to pray for him, even though they were separated by half a world ever since he went away to college. Her mortality was never far from her thoughts, as she battled cancer for over thirty years of her life. God was completely faithful to that prayer by keeping her health stable until December 1998, the month our actual dating relationship started.

Soon thereafter, another piece of mom Ferwerda's prayer puzzle emerged. Steve was rummaging through some papers and came across a birthday card from his mom dated May 1998, six months before we began our relationship. In it was just another reminder of answered prayer and another confirmation. "I am praying that God would give you the desires of your heart [for a wife] *this year.*" Her urgency for these prayers (aside from Steve's ripe old age) was a spiritual premonition of her upcoming departure. What joy to see these heartfelt prayers answered and to know she knew it and accepted me before she died.

It is a great loss to me that I did not get the chance to meet this larger-than-life woman personally, although I have gotten to know her through the many rich character qualities she influenced in Steve's life. Still, I feel as if she is a big part of my life and my love for God, because all those years across the world she prayed *for me.* That thought is so awesome to me. I only wish to have gotten the chance to tell her how much she has directly and indirectly blessed my life.

Dad Ferwerda as well contributed many wonderful traits into the life of his son that make him who he is today. Dad is a very tenderhearted man who has always been a devoted husband and father. One of my favorite traits that Dad imparted to Steve was doing the dishes. Steve remembers his Dad doing dishes frequently through the years to serve his wife in a practical manner. I am so blessed that Steve "caught" that wonderful serving trait! How loved a wife feels when her husband serves her in those every day tasks.

Likewise, all of Steve's family has extended grace and love to me, in spite of how differently we've arrived at this place in our lives. Their response to our relationship and marriage has been an incredible example of grace and acceptance. I can't forget to mention in particular, the incredible influence of his sister, Ruth Anne, and her painstaking instruction on such big sister things like crocheting. Those afghans will come in handy over long winter months spent in Wyoming.

P.M.S. (Post-Marriage Syndrome)

One night not so long ago my husband and I were sitting across from each other at the dining room table, each engrossed in our own computer projects—he into tasks for work, me working on editing this book. Reading up to the part about Steve giving me the last piece of the puzzle to be placed, I was overcome with emotion. I went over to where he was working, sat down on his lap and buried my face in his shoulder.

"What's wrong honey?"

"I'm just so happy!" I sobbed, soaking his white shirt with black mascara.

"You are? What are you so...*happy* about?"

"About the day you asked me to be your wife. I get so amazed every time I read it. It was one of the ha..ha..happpiest days of my life! I love you so much."

He gingerly pulled back to look into my black-streaked face and said very sweetly, "Honey, are you in P.M.S.?"

For your sake I will not keep silent, my child, till your justice shines out like the dawn, your salvation like a blazing torch. You will be a crown of splendor in My hand. No longer will you be deserted or desolate. People will hear me say, "My delight is in her, she is my bride." For the Lord will take delight in you, as a bridegroom rejoices over his bride, so will your God rejoice over you. Isaiah 62:1-5 (Paraphrased)

Endnotes

Chapter 3

1. Hannah Hurnard, Hinds Feet on High Places, (Wheaton, IL: Tyndale House Publishers, Inc., 1975), 104-105.
2. Oswald Chambers, My Utmost for His Highest, (Grand Rapids, MI.: Oswald Chambers Publications Association, Ltd., 1963), 15.
6. Beth Moore, Breaking Free: Making Liberty in Christ a Reality in Life, (Nashville: LifeWay Press, 1999), 22.

Did you enjoy this book? Please give it a rating on Amazon!

We also welcome feedback. Find out what we have been up to since our perfect day.

Visit www.JulieFerwerda.com.

www.ingramcontent.com/pod-product-compliance
Lightning Source LLC
Chambersburg PA
CBHW051650040426
42446CB00009B/1069